Helen,

25.12.86

Happy Christmas,

Love

Rosemary
xx

To remind you of <u>our</u>
schooldays at St. Felix!!

GIGGLING IN
THE SHRUBBERY

ARTHUR MARSHALL was educated at a Hampshire prep school, at Oundle and at Christ's College, Cambridge. He was a master and housemaster at Oundle from 1931 until 1954, departing only to join the Intelligence Corps during the war. After serving as private secretary to Lord Rothschild he became a full-time journalist and broadcaster in 1964. He has written for the *Sunday Telegraph*, *Punch*, the *Listener*, *The Times Literary Supplement*, the *New Statesman*, the *London Standard* and the *Spectator*. He is the author of several books, including the boys' companion to this volume, *Whimpering in the Rhododendrons*, and an autobiography, *Life's Rich Pageant* (both available in Fontana).

Giggling in the Shrubbery

The splendours and miseries
of girls' boarding schools
as recalled by former pupils

Edited by
ARTHUR MARSHALL

Drawings by Tim Jaques

FONTANA/COLLINS

First published in Great Britain
by William Collins Sons & Co. Ltd 1985
First issued in Fontana Paperbacks 1986

Made and printed in Great Britain by
William Collins Sons & Co. Ltd, Glasgow

Contents

Foreword

GIRLS! Girls everywhere! Girls in the passages, girls
in the hall, racing upstairs and scurrying downstairs,
diving into dormitories and running into classrooms,
overflowing on to the landing and hustling along the
corridor – everywhere, girls! There were tall and short,
and fat and thin, and all degrees from pretty to plain;
girls with pigtails and girls with flowing hair, blue-
eyed, brown-eyed, and grey-eyed girls; demure girls,
romping girls, clever girls, stupid girls – but never a
silent girl. No! Buzz-hum-buzz!

Although this spirited and vivid piece of prose could be a
description of almost any girls' boarding school anywhere in
Britain and at any point in the last eighty or so years (or does
the mention of pigtails date it a little?), it comes in fact from
The School by the Sea and from the distinguished pen of who else
but Miss Angela Brazil. The book was a First World War
offering to her ever widening circle of devoted schoolgirl
readers and it is notable for having a particularly jolly and
unusual type of Headmistress, Miss Birks; 'a strain of Irish in
her genealogy had given her the pleasant twinkle in the eye,
the racy humour of speech, and the sunny optimistic view of
life'.
   The passage quoted above opens the story and finds the girls,
a 'frolicsome crew' indeed, reassembling after the Christmas

holiday, the Head taking an indulgent view of the noisy hustle and bustle ('Let them fizz, poor dears!'). Miss Birks is forty-five years old, possesses 'undoubted brain power', reacts sympathetically when Dulcie Wilcox comes over faint during algebra, tells humorous Irish stories and is apt to dose invalids with 'a harmless mixture of Turkey rhubarb and carbonate of magnesia'. You'll want to know to whom Miss Birks awarded the coveted General Improvement Prize. It went to Gerda Thorwaldson, wrongly suspected of being a German spy (it was, after all, 1914).

That, however, is as far as we go in the field of fiction, for in the pages that follow it is facts that we are after, facts supplied in full measure by a gallant band of women who, invited to cast their minds back to their own days at school, have provided a fascinating and splendidly varied flood of memories. A list of these benefactors will be found at the end of the book and our gratitude goes to them for the trouble they have taken. It was cheering to discover that, by and large, the majority of Old Girls, if I may so call them, look back on their schooldays with amusement and on the school staffs with affection.

1

Headmistresses

The list of famous Headmistresses is a long and impressive one for it contains the names of Dame Emmeline Tanner, Miss Buss, Miss Beale, Miss Reader Harris and Miss Lawrence of Roedean (enormously fat and very vain about her hats) and it is of course only right and proper that we should begin our survey with the one person that really matters at a girls' school, the Headmistress. And so let us start with a recollection of a jolly, roly-poly sort of educational force from the early 1920s.

I absolutely adored our Headmistress. We called her Bunjie, goodness only knows why, and she was in many ways so like my mother, though not in looks for she was plump and dumpy and what Americans call 'homely' (polite word for 'plain'). Her clothes were a complete disgrace and could have gone straight into a Jumble Sale (buyers doubtful) but she had such a way with her. She used to rush about shrieking 'Get busy' at anybody who was for one moment idle. It was quite a small school so we got to know her well. We all loved her. It wasn't the usual kind of silly 'crush' but a motherly thing really, I suppose. On summer evenings when she wasn't too busy we were allowed to come down in our dressing-gowns and sit about and gossip and munch biscuits.

Not all school evenings ended so agreeably. One of Nancy Spain's many hilarious party pieces was to describe and act the bedtime ritual at her extremely large school. It seems the Headmistress ruled that every night ('Good night, Nancy. Good night, Monica') every girl ('Good night, Nancy. Good night, Jessica') had to shake hands ('Good night, Nancy. Good night, Maureen') with every school prefect ('Good night, Nancy. Good night, Cynthia') as they wound their way ('Good night, Nancy. Good night, Prudence') upstairs to bed. A fellow sufferer remembers a nightly procedure of a similar grimness.

> The school numbered between three and four hundred girls and EVERY NIGHT each one was expected to bid good night to the Headmistress, Miss Black, or 'Ma' as we called her. She sat upon a chair with her feet on a foot stool while the school formed a queue around the large gymnasium. Each girl waited her turn, then was held by the right hand, stooped and kissed the cheek of the Head who said 'Good night, dear': the pupil replied 'Good night, Miss Black' and passed along. Any misbehaviour reported during the day was noted and at 'Good Night Time' the culprit was told to stand aside until the ritual was over; she was then coldly admonished and a suitable punishment was given.

But friendly evening gatherings can be very beneficial to all concerned provided, as here, the atmosphere is right.

> For a good many years I did some of the teaching myself but it soon became impossible to cope with all the writing and business as well. Headmistresses generally say that they can only get to know their pupils by teaching them but I found that I learned much more about them by seeing them at all sorts of odd times and specially when they were alone in the Sick Quarters. The girls could always come to me whenever they wished, and before supper every even-

ing a crowd came into the drawing-room and sat on the floor round my chair. The girls liked to hear my latest news and I thoroughly enjoyed theirs. It is amusing that children always think that you know nothing of any subject that you do not teach them. I took a Geography class when a teacher was ill and one small girl asked quite solemnly, 'Do you know any Geography?'

In many schools it was the Headmistress who took charge of religious instruction, which led in one case to a pleasing misunderstanding.

Our naïvety astounds me still. On Sunday afternoons we had an hour's session with the Headmistress. This particular class was known as B.U.R.P.S. As the topic was religion, I naturally assumed that the B stood for Bible and the S for Society. To clear up the wilderness of letters in the middle, I asked one of the school's original pupils, some years later, what in fact B.U.R.P.S. stood for. 'Burps?' she said. 'We called it burps because Miss Williams was always burping.'

Sometimes the religious instruction took place rather later in the day.

Miss Cooke seems to have impressed all who came in contact with her – staff, girls and townspeople – as a dignified, somewhat aloof person, demanding high standards in everything, quick to notice and to reprove untidiness or slovenliness, earnest and rather imperious. Yet she was a keen games enthusiast and an early member of the Women's Cricket Association. She taught the girls to question and to think for themselves and insisted that they make the best use of all their time at school. Her Old Girls report that they feared but admired her, and the parents found her charming. Certainly, her presence was over all in school and many ex-pupils still remember the ideas and ideals which she propounded in her Sunday evening talks. For instance, in one intriguingly original sermon she described a railway journey using the old regional lines – long before the days of British Rail. L.N.E.R. stood for Let Nothing Evil Remain; L.M.S. meant Love My School; G.W.R. – Grousing Without Reason and S was Selfishness! On another occasion, she impressed her hearers by criticising a line in the end-of-term hymn which goes 'Time that's lost may all retrieve'. She said that it was nonsense for lost time could *never* be retrieved.

Headmistresses are very seldom thrown off balance. They keep, as the current phrase goes, their cool, however trying the circumstances. At one time in my life when I was busily gathering information about girls' schools for literary purposes (rather too grand a description of my activities) I was being shown round a prosperous and well regarded school by the Headmistress, Miss Brakewell. She was everything that one could wish for in my particular field – tall, spare, highly awe-inspiring and completely humourless. We had visited the sanatorium where girls lying ill in bed all sat smartly up at the sight of Miss Brakewell, as though each had been jerked upright by some powerful spring. Wandering through the kitchen garden we had come upon two terrified juniors entangled in the raspberry canes and busily helping themselves ('Come and report to me after Prayers'). As we made our way round the premises Miss Brakewell's theme song was the importance of orderliness. 'A place for everything and everything in its place.' Otherwise all in a school was chaos. For instance, she said, at the end of the long passage down which we were progressing lay the Macintosh Cupboard. In it the girls hung their macintoshes and their school hats. There were numbered pegs, each with its macintosh. One girl, one macintosh. Thus, every girl knew where she was. At the very slightest hint of inclement weather, all made a bee line for the

Macintosh Cupboard and the numbered pegs. By now we had arrived at the cupboard and Miss Brakewell flung the door proudly open. I peered excitedly within, expecting a sea of macintoshes. There were, however, no numbered pegs at all. There were no macintoshes. There were no hats. But the cupboard was not empty. It contained just the one item – a very large lawnmower. This at least, I thought, must 'throw' my conductor, but not at all. 'There has evidently been some little administrative rearrangement,' said Miss Brakewell without a tremor, and she sailed serenely onwards.

As many will recall, although parental visits to schools were looked forward to for weeks ahead, they often held moments of acute embarrassment.

> One glorious summer day, when the school was to per-
> form the annual Shakespeare play, my mother arrived,
> an enchanting floating trailing vision with some *dernier*
> *cri* escort in tow who was definitely not Daddy.
>
> 'Oh, Miss England!' she cried on encountering that
> dignitary, 'how are you? And how is darling Baba?'
>
> 'Barbara, I regret to say, is an extremely tiresome
> little girl. I only hope that in time we can improve
> her.'
>
> 'Oh, but Miss England!' cried my mother, fluttering
> long gloves, feather-boa, eyelashes and parasol, all
> together. 'You mustn't make her *too* good . . . or no
> one will ever want to marry her!'
>
> '*That*, Mrs Allen,' said Miss England, *trampling the*
> *butterfly underfoot*, 'will be *quite* the least of my future
> worries.'
>
> On a more distressing occasion, my mother visited
> me, and as soon as she arrived I discerned all the
> signs of a maternal exhortation. Finding me a healthy
> red-faced lump, she voiced her disapproval in no uncer-
> tain terms.
>
> 'Really, Barbara! When I think of what Daddy
> spends on your education . . . And what is the result?

My mother arrived, an enchanting, floating, trailing vision, with some *dernier cri* escort in tow . . .

You can't dance, you can't sing, you can't play the piano, you won't be musical or graceful, you can't even recite or act, you do nothing to make yourself attractive, you have spots on your chin and *you won't wear stays . . .*'

Stung beyond bearing by this all-too-true assessment, I mumbled defiantly, 'Well, anyway, I won the quarter-mile last sports-day, and won it jolly well.'

'My good child,' said maternal scorn, 'don't add being a perfect little fool to everything else. You can't win a husband by getting up and running round the drawing-room!'

And that was by no means the end of poor Barbara's troubles.

There was no twinkle in Miss England's eye when I returned for my last year, as a prefect. During the holidays my mother, still motivated by her match-making impulses, had decided that I should look better with the prevailing new fashion of bobbed hair instead of a heavy straggling plait. As a prefect it would be incumbent on me to put up my hair every evening, and for once I was entirely in agreement with her that it would not be a becoming performance.

To the hairdresser, therefore, we had gone and, except for a moment when, seeing me half shorn, my mother had given a piercing cry, 'Oh, darling! I don't think I like it after all,' the operation had been success-fully carried out; and I, rejoicing alike in the delectable lightness and freedom of my head, and in the vast improvement in my appearance, was as proud as a peacock.

'And *what*,' inquired Miss England, meeting me in the front hall, 'have you done to your hair?'

'I've had it bobbed, Miss England,' said I, looking up at her from under my page-boy fringe and giving the whole aureole an imperceptible swing.

She eyed me with disgust, all the more aggravated because, short of expelling me, there was nothing she could do about it; but she crushed me to the earth.

'Barbara,' she said, 'not only do you look indescr-r-rib-ably *vulgar*, but you have disgraced the Honour of the Sixth Form!' And she swept onwards.

But I, puffed up with the intoxication of my newly-apprehended beauty, was deliriously above myself. I was so far gone that I even took a squint down the years ahead and caught a glimpse of a really not-too-bad husband after all.

A strict Headmistress is an alarming spectacle and, oddly enough, never more so than when she decides from time to time to remove the mask, graciously unbend, and become momentarily jolly.

Very occasionally one was invited for a purely social visit to the Head's drawing-room. It was a beautiful room, light and chintzy, full of flowers, floor-to-ceiling windows that opened on to a long covered verandah overlooking the sea a hundred feet below. There was a shiny black Bechstein in one corner, a repository for countless photographs of Old Girls Who Had Succeeded – some by marrying well, most of them in long white dresses, white ostrich feathers in their hair, smug and well-groomed for their presentation at Court. It was of course assumed that one knew what was meant by 'Being Presented' – and if one didn't, one held one's tongue and found out in the next letter home.

Afternoon tea with the Head was an excruciating privilege; ink-stained fingers clasped fragile Worcester china, plates were balanced precariously on shaking knees while the Head, with unaccustomed bonhomie, asked after your little sister or your summer holiday or the piece you were playing at the end-of-term concert.

The parlour maid, Christabel, a craggy Scotswoman

well into her forties, served the tea, her face expression-less as she handed round cucumber sandwiches, passed the bread and butter, placed the cakestand where we were least likely to knock it over. We were used to seeing her in the Dining Hall, controlling our natural greed with as much authority as the Head herself – but now, in these highly civilised surroundings, she was the perfect maidservant, cap and pinny an' all, never suggesting by so much as a flicker of an eyelid that we rated one jot less than the dearest of the Head's contemporaries.

Once outside, liberated from the previous hour's corset-like restraint, well out of earshot, we'd run shrieking down the Library Corridor, laughing and giggling, exclaiming, 'My dear, it was GHASTLY! I nearly spilt the LOT! And you should have seen her FACE!' – and Christobel would nod and wink at us, and tell us we'd best 'shut that clamour before *She* gets to hear ye'.

Considerable courage was needed by those girls who, deciding that they had a legitimate grievance, stood up to the Head-mistress.

I had a couple of skirmishes with Miss Jacobs myself, in one I was victorious, in the other she was. Honours were even.

The first skirmish was about dried peas. One of the extraordinary things we were given for supper was dried peas, cooked, certainly, but unadorned in any way and with nothing to eat with them. Best not to go into the results of a meal consisting entirely of dried peas, enough to say that we very soon noticed that they turned the forks black, and if the forks, then, we all assumed, our stomachs. So, urged on by me, we refused to eat them and I was sent for to the study.

'Why do you refuse to eat the dried peas?' enquired

'J' majestically. I explained about the black forks and the conclusion we had drawn from them.

'The peas are perfectly wholesome,' said Miss Jacobs. 'Now when I was at school we had bad fish every Friday but no one complained and no one *ever* told their parents. What do you think of that?'

Well, I could have told her, but self-preservation kept my lips sealed. I was dismissed with a caution, but for the rest of the time I was at the school we never had dried peas again.

In the second confrontation I was not successful. It was the custom, or rather the rule, that on packing day at the end of term all our clothes had to be mended, and before they were packed Miss Jacobs (how busy she must have been!) inspected everything. Now, in my last year I was seventeen and Mother, who by that time – for I am going ahead of myself a bit – was back in South Africa, gave me a dress allowance of £5 a month and I bought my own clothes. So, my four pairs of black woollen stockings being absolutely worn out and due to be thrown away as soon as I arrived at whichever aunt was having me those holidays, I did not trouble to mend them. Miss Jacobs inspected and pounced.

'These stockings are in holes,' she said. I explained the situation but she wouldn't have it.

'Mend them!' she ordered.

I spent most of that day mending black stockings and each time I took them to the study for inspection she ran a finger down the toes and broke through my darns. By the time night descended and I was allowed to pack, those stockings held together, but I gave them to my aunt's housemaid for cleaning rags as soon as I got home.

In some cases the courage to speak up was lacking.

Our Headmistress was a distinctly impressive lady,

who retained her dignity in all circumstances, in spite of the handicap of an almost perpetually red nose (brought about, I feel sure, by dyspepsia rather than the alcoholism at which some of our brasher school-mates hinted). The constant wearing of her gown (when other staff only sported them on Speech Days) added to her lordly air. I had a running battle with her almost from the moment I entered the school. I think that in her view the only acceptable form of movement for a girl was to glide or billow (as indeed she did herself). But with a tendency to be late for lessons through gossiping and giggling with my friends, I favoured running as a means of locomotion. I also had difficulty in keeping my hair tidy and my gymslip brushed – so, marked down as a hoyden, I was fre-quently on the receiving end of the Head's reforming and sarcastic quips. Of course I longed to answer back, but dare not – even when she frigidly remarked that I had an 'evil genius' for treating everyone as my contemporary and my equal (a quite unconscious talent on my part, by the way).

Although a tough disciplinarian, she was also sur-prisingly progressive. Amongst her many schemes for broadening our interests and sense of social respon-sibility was one for lending us out from time to time on community service projects. The (apparently un-ending) war was still on, and there was always a strong need for 'voluntary' schoolgirlish help. No-one could say that I excelled at these projects. I found uncon-genial the tasks demanded of me by the local nursing-home to which I (or rather the Head) had offered my occasional labours. Crudely dicing enormous piles of vegetables, washing up, 'Vimming' the knives and sluicing bedpans were not my forte, and the flame of Florence Nightingale flickered to a rapid standstill within my breast. I think at heart I was always an escapist, and I wanted my part in the war effort to be colourful and exciting. The same adjectives could be applied to a great deal of the sub-literature in which I wallowed during my schooldays. The Head was particularly concerned about what we read – and there was a wholesale banning from Brookfield of many types of reading matter (most of which we managed to find, circulate and relish). This ranged, I remember, from *Film Fun* and the *Girls' Crystal* at one extreme to *No Orchids for Miss Blandish* at the other.

For a really alarming Headmistress, let us go back fifty years and to a Dorset school.

I think it would be fair to say that for all except a handful of children who appeared to bask in her perpetual favour, to meet Miss Wilson was to experience a sense of doom, disaster, even despair!

The first time I met her was when my father took me to the school to collect a house tie and hat band. We were shown by a maid into the drawing-room and it was some time before Miss Wilson herself appeared. I recognised her immediately as the tall rawboned masculine figure resembling some Old Testament prophet, a cross between Elijah and Moses, that I had seen outside the school staff room.

She wore a severely tailored brown suit, skirt well below the knee, a cream-coloured blouse and green tie, men's woollen knee socks, brogues and a curious Trilby-type hat with a very wide brim. Her style of dress was unique to her. I had not even been sure whether she was a man or a woman.

Miss Wilson shook hands with Father and eyed me with undisguised disapproval, so that I was immediately conscious that my untidy fringe, not yet long enough to be held by a slide, was slipping out of its Kirby grips, and that one sock with a loose garter was slipping down my leg. I was ten years old and small for my age.

On my first day at the school, Miss Wilson was wearing an old tweed skirt and green woollen jersey, somewhat out at the elbow. Her unruly curly grey hair was awry and her steely blue-grey eyes looked piercingly at me from under thick jutting eyebrows. Both her eyes and her aquiline nose reminded me of an eagle preparing to rend its prey. Her mouth looked cruel and curled contemptuously at the corners. When lunchtime came, she gestured me, without speaking, to a vacant chair beside her. 'Plum,' she called to a pigtailed girl at the end of the table, 'say Grace.' 'For what we are about to receive may the Lord makes truly thankful.' A clatter of chairs and we all sat down.

Totally ignoring me, Miss Wilson cracked a series of corny jokes at which the school obediently tittered, interspersed with shouts of 'Mary, take your finger off the blade of your knife' and 'Joanna, wake up and pass the salt to Ann.' 'Mary, where was Moses when the light went out?' 'I don't know, Miss Wilson.' 'In the dark, you cuckoo.' More titters.

I regret to say that unflattering physical descriptions of Headmistresses abound.

—The Headmistress who, I believe, was quite a scholar, was tall, severe and middle-aged. She was whiskery, and her teeth were a poor fit. Her hair, grey and thinning, was parted in the centre with 'earphones' and she wore rimless pince-nez. I remember her in no other outfit than an ankle length Black Watch tartan kilt and a fawn cardigan.

—The Headmistress was a short but majestic woman with pince-nez, a large bust, and tiny feet like pigs' trotters.

—Our Headmistress prided herself on her 'iron will'. She was a strange-looking creature – dumpy, iron-grey hair and moustache. She always wore long, serge dresses with a train, and was unloved, and completely unforgiving.

—She mostly wore grey. I remember silky knitted jumpers and numerous long gold chains. At Assembly, if she had to report a misdemeanour, she would say 'I mention no names . . .' and then fix the culprit with a steely eye, leaving the smug onlookers in no doubt about 'Who'd dun it'! She had an ancestor who was one of the murderers of Thomas à Becket!

—Miss Boileau was really rather chic and smartly turned out. We didn't like her much and, looking back, I think we may all have been a bit jealous of her as she was still quite pretty and we all looked ghastly in our school clothes. She smelt of good scent (my sophisticated chum, Helen, said it was *'Arpège'*) and we all thought that she looked a bit like the then Lady Mountbatten. There were two persistent rumours about her. One was that she was the mistress of a Grand Duke (she seemed rather rich and was said to have been spotted at Boulogne with a tall man with a beard). The other rumour was that she drank, based on the fact that a prefect had once allegedly seen in her study a half empty bottle of Wincarnis. I'm sure that Wincarnis is delicious but it doesn't somehow quite fit into the Lady Mountbatten picture. Both rumours must have been bosh but we greatly enjoyed embroidering them.

—She was like half-a-dozen Margaret Rutherfords rolled into one, with great flowing capes swirling about, vast floppy hats with white hair bursting out from underneath, huge and voluminous purple skirts, and, when out of doors, an umbrella, even under a cloudless sky. She was a darling and nobody mocked her.

As is perhaps to be expected, some Headmistresses have, down the years, displayed some not very worrying eccentricities.

—Many of my recollections are of the splendidly eccentric Headmistress. A remarkable woman in many ways, although some of these ways were markedly strange. She was at her most unpredictable around the full moon. Probably coincidentally. She greeted one mother with a cry of 'Ho! Sir Francis Drake!' but as the lady was called Treasure one can see the connection. Before the Sixth Form dance the girls were warned of the terrible infection which could be caught from dancing 'too close – rubbin' cheeks', with the Boys' College contingent. Even with our rudimentary knowledge this seemed rather strong but she meant – what else? – acne. Her contribution to the festivities was to mingle, swatting, with cries of 'No babies! No babies!'

I remember passing her open study window one morning and hearing the deep county tones 'Good morning Little Egg. I'm going to chop your head off,' which, I suppose, displays more old world courtesy than the usual surprise attack. Which reminds me, one of the joys of prize-giving (The Winter Gardens, Jerusalem and a much practised form of formation marching) was the award of a Cup for Good Manners under Difficult Circumstances.

—On one occasion the Principal broke off in the middle of a conversation with some parents and said 'I must fly, your son is loose amongst my maidens' as she hurried off in pursuit.

—One simply didn't argue with the Headmistress. She burst into my (single) room late one night and woke me, bellowing 'No talking!' She then told me that sleeping with the window closed was most unhealthy (which was in fact the reason why mine was open a good nine inches) and closed it with a bang. She breezed out with a not unfriendly 'Such a naughty gel.' I was a moderately articulate sixteen-year-old by this time but remained silent and wide-eyed throughout. As I say, one simply did not argue.

—Miss Meadows had a simple way of dealing with parents' letters. She never answered them.

—She wore her hair in two braids drawn across her brow and, unusually in those days, eschewed the wearing of a brassiere. After I had left a few of the Senior girls went to tea with her, after which she leant back, stretched and admired the view with 'Oh girls, look at the tits!' Such was the coarsening of the young ladies by then that they did not immediately look at the bird-table.

—I remember that a minor infringement of a trivial school rule inspired her to call us 'second-class whores'. I wrote to my mother in high dudgeon. She replied equally indignantly 'With all the money we're paying you should be first-class by now.'

—The school was run by the Sisters of an Anglican order headed by Mother Mary, a small woman with a beak of a nose, penetrating brown eyes and a *glide* – she didn't walk. The adoration and veneration afforded by the nuns and novices and which we pupils were expected to show really stuck in my gullet. This Deity ate with the pupils in the refectory for Sunday lunch. Looking down the refectory table and seeing me, she asked 'What is the name of that new child who looks like a codfish?' Not only had my hair been cropped but I wore a plate on my front teeth to correct my 'Rabbit' teeth. All eyes were turned on me. I wanted to die.

—Her really manic rages were rare but oddly self-fuelling, usually stemming from some minor problem which in the course of the diatribe became symptomatic of all the evil in the world. I remember her talking in Assembly about the need to read exam questions carefully which, apparently, we had not been doing. The speech progressed from a reasoned discussion of examiners' requirements, to our future unemployability, to '. . . and if you do get married, you'll have children and they'll get sick and you'll read their medicine bottle labels wrongly and give them the wrong dose and kill them and I'll be glad, glad, GLAD!'

—Miss Hamilton's last words to me as I left school were 'Gain in self-control if you can and don't marry a Roman Catholic or a foreigner.' I didn't – I wouldn't have dared.

2

Accommodation

It has been claimed that provided children are happy, well fed and warm, they are quite oblivious to their surroundings and in some cases this is just as well. Nothing in boarding schools varies quite as much as the accommodation prepared for the inmates and it is usually accommodation that is being constantly added to (a new science wing: a hostel for junior mistresses: the Pankhurst Debating Room) or, though rarely, subtracted from. In this latter connection, I always felt at school that when Royalty kindly came down to open something, she should at the same time be required to close something unattractive, preferably by blowing it up ('. . . and now I will ask Her Royal Highness to close the original school lavatories', upon which the lady bends down and presses one of those plunger things and up goes Old Bogger in a cloud of dust and debris).

The greatest variations occur when schools have not begun as schools but are former country houses or mansions, skilfully (in some cases) converted into dormitories, classrooms, bathrooms and so on. These too grow, in time, wings and bunion-like excrescences for the construction of which reliance has often been placed on corrugated iron.

At the time, and it was roughly seventy years ago, when girls' boarding schools were springing up all over the place, the sea was considered to provide the ideal venue (Dr Brighton

and all that) and it is by the sea that we frequently find
ourselves.

Eastbourne in the 1930s was surely the heart of the
Girls' Boarding School industry and in due time sister
Sheila and I were despatched to a school – selected
not so much for its academic prowess as for its position,
perched high upon a steep incline on the seafront,
braced against the southerly gales like a four-masted
schooner, manned by as mixed a bag of maidens (and
in those days we were) as you could hope to find.

The magazine of the Headmasters' Conference was pleased to
report the following:

Felixstowe College is not by the sea or on the sea. It
is practically in it . . . A small lawn and a slender line
of tamarisks intervene and then the brown sea laps.
Ferries and tankers pass the window as if they were
buses in the street below. Beyond must lie the Dogger
Bank and beyond that Jutland.

However, schools that were not by the sea do not seem to have
considered themselves particularly deprived.

At about five o'clock in the January dusk, the train
drew into Sedbergh station. There a very junior mistress was waiting to organise our transport to school.
First we had to see our trunks and holdalls out of the
luggage van and assembled on the platform, to be
collected and delivered by the carrier. Then, with our
overnight suitcases, we were led to the White Hart
horse bus and bundled in. It was not a very long
ride, but, well out of the village, we came to a heavy
five-barred gate with 'Balliol School for Girls' in black
on the white paint. We were driven right up to the
house, scrambled down and entered a dimly-lit side

entrance. Then along a stone-paved passage, lined
with lockers, we came to the cloakroom . . . There a
large boiler gave a pleasant warmth. It heated some
pipes to warm the classrooms and provided hot water
to the two bathrooms for the girls and a slightly more
luxurious one for the staff – all of them! It also helped
to air the cloaks we would hang on our named pegs,
which we sought by the dim light of a fish-tail gas
burner and the lockers beneath, where our frequently
wet shoes would be stored. When we had removed our
shoes and put on slippers, from our little overnight
cases, we were shown the row of doors leading into
partitioned cubicles with very basic WCs for our use.

In some cases (and it is rather rare in the young) there is
appreciation of what were pleasant surroundings.

St John's was an attractive place. There were lovely
old forest trees bordering the main London road and
a drive led up to the house with gardens on either side
and a rather sloping tennis lawn. In front of the house
there was another lawn with old cedar trees, a copper
beech and a tulip tree. There were no playing fields
and no games other than tennis and croquet, but there
were swings and a see-saw in a separate courtyard.
The kitchen garden produced masses of fruit and vegetables, but was naturally out of bounds.

The part of the garden under the forest trees by the
road was always out of bounds. The story was handed
down that one frivolous young lady had carried on
clandestine interviews with a swain over the wall. He
wore white gloves and her name was 'Sweetie', which
was asking for trouble! The dogs' cemetery was in this
forbidden ground and there were quite a dozen graves
with headstones bearing the names of the departed
pets.

All dormitories were completely unheated. Each cubicle had a narrow iron 'Hospital' bed, with a thin, hard mattress, said to be very healthy for the young.

Although girls and women have, or so I am led to believe, an extra layer of fat concealed somewhere about their persons, it is lack of warmth that is remembered, time and time again.

> The school was built at the top of a high hill and was a tall converted Victorian house. We had coal fires in the classrooms but nowhere else, no carpets on any floors and linoleum in the bedrooms – each with about five girls to a room. The building was ICY in the winter and we all had bad chilblains. However, we all thrived and never caught any illnesses from the day girls. The food was good, but plain, and always second helpings – plenty of porridge and suet puddings. There was no choice of dishes, but because we did not have packets of crisps and other 'junk' foods in those days, we ate anything given to us.

Here is a country house conversion that seems not to rate quite the highest marks.

> The house would not be considered a very suitable one for a school in these days. The dining-room was in the basement, next to the kitchen. It had two long tables and there was only one window, though light was added by glass on one side showing an area which housed a number of canaries.
>
> There were obviously no bathrooms when my great-aunts took the house. Later, one was contrived in an alcove off the sewing maids' room in the basement. This had only a curtain instead of a door. Still later, when I was a schoolgirl, a really fine bathroom was added upstairs and every girl had a bath once a week, which was considered very modern.
>
> The drawing-room was very full of furniture. The sofa and chairs were covered with embossed velvet. There was one gold chair with a back shaped like a harp and the walls were completely covered with all sorts of pictures. One enormous one portrayed the wife

of Pontius Pilate coming down into the Judgment Hall and there was a grievous one of a dog stranded on some floating debris in a flood.

The drawing-room looked out on a verandah which had squares of glass in its floor, to light the area and the canaries, then came a lovely grass bank and the croquet lawn, and beyond that a large strawberry ground bordered, rather unwisely, by the girls' gardens. In the house there were two quite large classrooms, with long tables and very small hard chairs. These rooms were divided by folding doors and became one large room for Prayers and lectures. The very small room which was called the Governesses' Study was used for many other purposes and I cannot think what became of the staff, for they certainly never had a free day or free time.

The bedrooms were really the best part of the school but the furniture was hideous – black iron bedsteads and wooden chests and washstands painted yellow with red lines and ornamentation. All the walls were papered and I remember lying in bed and trying to work out the patterns. I have gone on to the third generation but I am sure that nothing in those bedrooms changed between 1857 and 1891 – certainly the beds remained with iron laths across and what I believe are called paliasses – hard as rocks. The cloakroom was called 'the pump room' because there was an enormous water tank under it. I have heard of one like it recently, in an old house, when some boards gave way and an unfortunate woman was suspended by one hand over terrifying depths of water. (She was rescued!)

The boot-basket must have lasted for generations. It was shallow and square and had straight-up sides. An 'old girl' of between sixty and seventy wrote recently that she remembered 'everything, even the boot basket'. It could have told a tale of elastic-sided boots and then button boots, followed by lace boots. But it had disappeared when we got down to shoes and giddy things like wellingtons. A window in the passage leading to the pump room had a long wooden tray on the ledge and here pencils were sharpened for some fifty years and I expect that this ledge was a rendezvous for the damsels in crinolines, just as it was in my day, as an excuse for respite from dull 'prep'.

And again . . .

Bussage House was, and still is, a curious building. Built against steeply rising ground it is three storeys high in the front and on ground-level at the back. It started life as a boys' school and Miss Beale and Miss Johnston had acquired it in about 1918. On the ground floor was the Hall, where we had our meals and Prayers were said morning and evening, the drawing-room, Miss Beale's domain, and the study which was Miss Johnston's lair and from where she pretty well ran the whole show. On the first floor were two classrooms and what was known as the Big Room, which was about the size of a small village hall. Here the whole social life of the school went on and it was used for classes as well, portable desks being carried about and set up wherever needed. The cloakroom and bath-rooms were on this level and on a sort of mezzanine floor were Miss Johnston's bedroom and a dormitory. The whole of the top, or attic floor, was divided into small dormitories by wooden partitions about six feet high, and these were divided again by curtains on rods. Each cubicle contained an iron bedstead and a combination washstand and dressing table. Each dormitory had different coloured bedspreads and cur-tains and were called Three Pink, Four Blue and so on. The staff, all very young, very inexperienced and very much under Miss Johnston's thumb, were stowed away in odd corners. They were all Ladies. As well as the Lady Gardener there was a Lady Cook, a Lady Matron and, inevitably, Mam'selle.

One school managed to take some of the drudgery out of housework.

One of my most vivid memories was of the old part of the school which had been a medium sized Regency family house. A beautiful panelled hall with stained glass windows and patterned tiled floor was always immaculate and highly polished. It is one of the rules of convents that they are always kept in perfect order. Before the days of electric polishers the nuns who didn't teach, but did the housework, used to strap a large square brush on one foot and use it as a sort of skate. They were very good at it and I'm sure that the exercise must have been excellent for the health temporal.

In one school we find a rather curious preprandial custom.

The building appeared to be a huge square block, but in the centre there was a large oak-panelled hall on the first floor with a domed glass roof and long galleries on either side on the floor above. Later a minstrels' gallery was added at one end. There was an imposing oak staircase from the entrance hall, used only by staff and prefects, which led to the hall and classrooms leading off it. Before meals the whole school assembled in the hall and 'walked round' until the bell rang for us to line up to go down to the dining-room. We walked arm in arm with one, two or three friends and caught up with the latest gossip.

It gave us an opportunity to let off steam and stretch our legs after sitting at our desks and to gaze at our current heroine from afar. As a new girl I sat and watched in amazement, quite deafened by the noise of a hundred walking, talking girls. There was one very kind girl who used to invite each of the new girls in turn to walk round with her. She had suffered a great deal; first she lost her mother, then her little sister fell off a haystack and was killed and finally her father was mauled by a panther in India and she herself had been badly burnt and scarred as a small child, so she was very sensitive to the feelings and needs of other people.

Here is another happy and appreciative boarder.

The school had lovely grounds with a great many trees. A cotton poplar caused a lot of trouble when it shed its cotton and made the tennis courts very slippery. There was an avenue of lime trees known as the red path, where we spent break, without having to change our shoes. In the summer when the lime flowers were in bloom the trees were alive with bees. On really hot days we sometimes had lessons out of doors, each sitting in our own deck chair. These chairs also came out on Sunday afternoons for 'Silence Hour'. We found a corner with a friend in the big hall, wrapped ourselves in rugs and sucked our twopennyworth of sweets and learnt the collect (and for seniors the epistle as well). These had to be recited later at Bible class. Sweets were ordered on Fridays, we could order two different kinds for our 2d. I used to have a bar of Sharp's toffee and some liquorice gums; some people would spend the whole 2d on a whipped cream walnut or bar of milk chocolate! The sweets came in separate little bags, each bearing our name and our order. I wonder what confectioner would take on the job now?

In British schools, even to this day, heating in dormitories is something of a rarity. Many in authority would consider it 'unhealthy' and productive of softies, but once more, lack of warmth is a chilly memory.

We, as the youngest members of the school, slept in the Green Dormitory – a large bedroom in the Headmistress's part of the house. The walls and paint were a good, serviceable green, and the floor was plain, scrubbed boards. The room was divided into seven cubicles by skimpy chintz curtains drawn along a framework of rods. The room must at some time have been a lovely bedroom in a private house, which this end of the school represented. There was a large fireplace, now blocked, to allow for another bed to be fitted in, and there was a small dressing-room off it, now occupied by the dormitory mistress. Each cubicle had a narrow iron 'hospital' bed, with a thin, hard mattress, said to be very healthy for the young. There was also a white, painted chest of drawers, with a basin and ewer on it. Under each bed was a shallow, painted metal bath and an enamel chamber pot. And alongside each bed was a small piece of carpet. There was a large, communal wardrobe cupboard near the door. On the bed was a thin under blanket, a sheet, one thin pillow, a top sheet and two thin blankets. All the beds had white, honeycomb covers, but these had to be removed at night, folded carefully, and placed on the chair at the foot of the bed. We were expected to bring with us a good travelling rug for cold weather! I found myself waiting anxiously for the arrival of my holdall with my rug!

In general a fairly cheerless picture emerges of dormitory life.

All dormitories were completely unheated, so healthy and so cold that frequently in winter the water in our ewers had slivers of ice floating in them. Many nights of that winter I only slept fitfully because I could not get warm. Grannie sent us each a pair of knitted bed stockings, which caused furious criticism from our dormitory mistress, but we were allowed to wear them after suggestions that they should be sent back!

Some random recollections of accommodation and other matters.

—Down the passage (tiled floor, loud clacking feet always, always) was the library, a shell of quietness. A gravy brown room with a smoky air, though probably not more than half a dozen cigarettes had ever been smoked in it. Across the half-glass door a cosy dark green curtain was slung and there was a window seat beneath the tall thin Victorian windows, which never admitted much light. At one end of the room was a gas fire and on Saturday mornings relays of girls knelt in front of this to dry their washed hair to a frizzle. For the rest, walls of books, tall chairs round the table and great blocks of card indexes. The rule of the library was silence. We could only speak about taking out a book, or in dire emergency. The nice thing about all this silence – it was fairly well kept – was that because of it you were classless. Outside its doors you were stamped – junior, senior, bad girl, lousy singer or whatever. But once in the library you, aged twelve searching for a Georgette Heyer, came into glorious harmony with a school prefect in her encyclopaedia or the history mistress in her Rousseau. It was like a no man's land in which everybody respected the importance of everyone else.

—There must have been about sixty boarders, of which I was the youngest. We slept in large dormitories with between ten and twenty in each. There was no heating and the water in the ewers, our sponges and other washing equipment frequently froze at night. Cold lino covered the floors. We each had an iron bed with heavy school blankets, a small shared bedside locker and one drawer. Each dormitory had one wardrobe in which our hanging garments and hats were kept.

—No child nowadays would endure the cold upstairs, though downstairs we had roaring log fires in the hall and common rooms. Food played a very important part in our lives. There is no doubt about it. We were extremely well fed, though we grumbled like mad about the meals.

—My boarding school days are as vivid in my memory as if they were last year.

I was at a private boarding school at Weston-super-Mare from 1930 to 1937.

Life was pretty spartan there, but then my upbringing could be called spartan, compared with today! At school I can remember constant chilblains on fingers and toes, except in the blissful summer term . . . No Hot Water Bottles for us – (but then, I didn't have one at home either, except in extreme illness such as measles).

—One of the joys of the Patricia was that we had a real fire, with a high guard; and as my nestlings were any age from seven to ten, a real nursery warmth still lingered in the cheerful glow. We were under the nominal care of an under-matron who left us entirely to our own devices, for she was far too pretty not to have plenty on her mind apart from us. Only every now and then she moaned because when any of them went to the loo in the middle of the night, the door handle screeched harsh and strident, defying all oiling.

'Couldn't you just *close* the door?' she would murmur plaintively, 'and not *shut* it? Anyway, who's going to besiege you in there at that hour?' But the nestlings were shocked at such an indecent suggestion and ground away at the handle as though its very noise protected their modesty.

—My next bed-sitting-room, though that perhaps is not a wholly accurate description, was a chaste and spartan cell on Top Storey at school. This coveted solitude was achieved for me by my mother because, having had curvature of the spine for several years, I was still considered delicate and was to be under observation for the present; but by the end of my first term there was no question of my being moved as strong women blenched at the thought of anyone so naughty being let loose in a dormitory.

—The Headmistress is still alive and well, aged about ninety-two and living in London. The school no longer exists but the house was bought by Victor Lowndes as a Training Centre for Bunny girls!!

3

Staff

The best way of describing staff practices and problems is to let a Headmistress speak for herself (some members of school staffs will relish the sideways swipe at gym mistresses).

It is impossible for outsiders to realize how many people a Headmistress must consider and try to please – parents, pupils, Old Girls, teachers, men and maids. Even after long experience there is always more to learn. The staff room in any school could tell queer tales. It is such an unnatural life for a crowd of women to live together and, unless they have outside friends and interests, it can be a very narrow existence. It is difficult for the Head to decide how much or how little contact is wise. The ideal surely is to interfere as little as possible and yet to make the mistresses feel that they will always have sympathy and a hearing about their own affairs, as well as school concerns. It was good to hear from a young matron after she left that she had always felt that 'there was a friend as well as a Headmistress in the study'. I know of one school where the Head is only accessible from 2 p.m. for twenty minutes and the approach to her room is like the pool of Bethesda and only those close to the door can get through it.

Staff meetings were friendly and informal. We always went through the names of all the girls and it was intriguing to hear quite contrary comments about the same child from different points of view.

Teachers have just as many queer ways for the Headmistress to cope with as the girls have. Each one thinks her subject is the most important of all and so she should, but quite often one must step in to keep the balance. Gym and games mistresses are the most persistent and girls would be drilling all day before any display unless someone protested.

The other side of the picture – a characteristic schoolgirl comment.

My recollections of schooldays tend to focus on small acts of rebellion simply because these were, in the main, only tiny bubbles in a vast ocean of conformity. Basically we were obedient and amenable schoolgirls; we respected our teachers, even when we passed round rude caricatures of them, and we were grateful for the dedication with which they listened to our troubles, guided us through the awful intricacies of algebra, made history from Ancient Sumeria to the suffragettes come tremendously alive, and stimulated our petty little spirits into passionate appreciation of the splendours of English poetry. And how they uplifted us with music! I still remember great groups of us almost bursting our lungs with exhilaration as we tackled tricky sections of 'The Messiah', 'St Patrick's Breastplate' and – of course – 'Forty Years On'.

Three more friendly opinions.

—I went to an absolutely marvellous boarding school: Elmhurst Ballet School. Before I was lucky enough to win a scholarship there, it had always been my fantasy school. I was an avid reader of *Girl* comic (with parental approval) and *Girls Crystal* and all the others secretly. It was extraordinary that although I am sure the majority of their readers didn't go to boarding schools, these magazines were full of stories about girls who did. 'Belle of the Ballet' was the story in *Girl* that caught my imagination, and when I went to Elmhurst the reality nearly mirrored my fantasy.

We actually did have a head ballet teacher with grey hair in a bun who hit our legs with a stick if our pliés were not up to standard. Bliss! We also had to curtsey to her – and indeed all teachers when we met them in the grounds. In fact when I went to my first audition after leaving school, the choreographer told me that she could always recognise Elmhurst girls because they came on stage and curtseyed. This, incidentally, was only twenty-five years ago.

—The staff were women whose price was above rubies, for those were the golden days when teaching meant a vocation and a dedication. The confining shackles of Victorian prejudice, which considered teaching the only suitable profession for so many unsuitable women, had vanished for ever. The ruthless search for self-expression, and the relentless selfishness which considered teaching as just another job to be exploited as far as possible, were yet unknown. These women of inspired ideals, shining intellect and thorough conscientious training, had the singular conception, the curious conviction, that the hearts and bodies, souls and minds of growing girls were among the most precious gifts that God had given to England; they even had hidden and sacred thoughts about the wives and mothers of the future.

—I think the staff were under nearly as much discipline as the girls and had very little freedom or comfort. Some of their rooms were on the top floor opposite the practising cubicles and the jangling noise was awful all afternoon and evening. They had all qualified at a university, at their own expense, and in a girls' boarding school had little opportunity of meeting men and most of them never married. I only remember one who became engaged while she was at the school. There was also a great shortage of eligible men after the enormous casualties of the First World War. What we hated most was sarcasm from the staff, and when there was trouble to be told that if we behaved like that they could only wonder what sort of homes we came from! On the whole they were a splendid lot of people doing a very demanding job for very little pay.

Unkind behaviour seems, and for both sexes, to be an inseparable part of growing up, as this appalling confession shows.

We were dreadfully cruel but only to staff, not each other. The cleaner, whose name was Mrs Liffey, had the most appalling BO, so of course we called her Whiffy Liffey. When we went into our classroom in the morning, it would be, as it were, filled with her presence. We did awful things like writing BO on the blackboard, and leaving bottles of Mum rollette where she would find them. It never made any difference.

Another victim of our cruelty was a housemistress, who I now think was not very mentally stable. When she left the school she was even less so. When she joined us she had come from a girls' reformatory, and told us she was looking forward to dealing with young ladies. I'm afraid she was to be sadly disappointed. We set out to drive her mad and I think we nearly did. One of the dining tables had extending leaves, and while she was not looking, we would push the two outer leaves in, so that she would see a small table with the girls crowded round it. Then we would extend the leaves and the next time she looked she would see a large table. When she came to say goodnight to us, with another housemistress, we would all call out goodnight to the other housemistress, and ignore her, as if she wasn't there. She had a terrible mangy dog which would come into the dining-room with her, and we would get it under a table, and balance it on our feet, so that she would think it had disappeared. She decided to get us interested in basket weaving, and we discovered that if you lit the cane you could smoke it. We were doing this once, and she came in, watched, and left the room. I decided that she knew it to be fatal, and was hoping we would all poison ourselves.

When we had our end of term fancy dress party, I dressed up in a terrible parody of this poor woman, while another, very small, girl went as her dog.

For some strange reason and in almost all schools, those who teach French, whether they be natives or not, are nearly always objects of mockery and derision. In schoolgirl fiction they fare equally badly, but the following examples are from life.

—It wasn't long after the end of the Great War and many of us were convinced that our small dark-skinned French mistress was really a German. She was known as 'Fritz'.

There was a flat-footed waitress with a lugubrious expression and fuzzy hair. Naturally she was known as 'Fuzzy'. It was the height of hilarity when Fritz at dinner after the rare treacle tart, called in a loud voice, 'Fuzzy, I will 'ave some more!' Humour was simpler in those days.

—One day the games mistress was late for her class. Mademoiselle was furious and slammed the door, saying she would drill us.

Her first order was 'Feet on 'ips and 'ands down.' Quite impossible and it was hard not to laugh. Then we had to run round the room while she said, 'Allez, Allez Hup' then 'Hup, Hup, Hup. Repeat.' There were endless stories of her eccentricities, but she was kind to us.

—A French mistress once sent down word that she was dying and I found her gasping on her bed. I hastily summoned the doctor, but I noticed that, in the interval, she had been well enough to get up and place a fetching blue bow on her nightdress, so my anxiety abated.

—The staff were every bit as mixed as the girls they taught. One or two were quite brilliant, like the writer of crime fiction, Miss R, who appeared each week on a one-day visit, dressed in hand-embroidered smock and amber beads; her face set in the Sitwell mould, she taught us to draw and paint. So well did she teach that more than an average number of us did actually become painters. There was 'Popeye', who could make French interesting, who was also a writer of successful novels, who could paint the scenery and sew the costumes for the plays she wrote, produced and directed, and who had a Siamese cat, James, taken everywhere with her on the end of a pale blue leather lead. She – Popeye – terrified the daylights out of us, but we admired her and sometimes we almost liked her.

Another teacher shared our admiration for Popeye, trailing round the school in her wake very much like James; poor unattractive adenoidal D-W, she had so little going for her, never mind the stink of nicotine that enveloped her, but she knew her stuff, and if we giggled at the funny dresses she wore to Saturday evening dances, played her up in class, even so we listened when she taught and we learned a lot.

—I 'came down' from St Hilda's, Oxford, in June 1901 and was looking forward to a really long summer holiday before starting work in September, but there was a crisis at St John's over a French mistress and I was summoned to take over the French teaching

for the second half of the term. One of the girls had
so exasperated Mademoiselle that she slapped her
in public and the French lady returned to her native
land. The girl in question was terribly hot-tempered
and uncontrolled. During that same term she was
made to apologise for some rudeness and I heard
her dash up to her bedroom, seize her water bottle
and fling it across the room at the opposite wall to
vent her wrath.

One of the chief events of each term was the
'Concours'. Each girl had a book of French words
and had to learn ten of them each day. This
amounted to a very considerable vocabulary by
the end of term when the French master solemnly
questioned the assembled school. As girls failed to
answer they left their place till only one girl remained
and received a prize. These 'petits mots', as we
called them, have often come in useful. On one visit
to Bruges, an Englishwoman rushed out of a shop
and asked if I could tell her the French for poker. I
knew its exact place and page in the word book but
I am sure that otherwise it would never have come
my way. St John's girls could have held their own
with any school in French and I have always enjoyed
airing mine, especially in long motor tours through
France.

The girls had French classes every day, so I was
kept busy understudying Monsieur Marrot and I
also taught history and literature. The elder girls
were only about four or five years younger than I
was and they were accustomed to make a point of
getting sent out of class for bad behaviour and then
going off into the garden till the next lesson. I
surprised them by condemning them to remain
present but on hard lockers at the back of the room
and their nonsense soon stopped.

—Miss Turvey – nicknamed 'Topsy', what else? –

came to us from Budleigh Salterton, a healthy, busty woman in her late thirties who was invariably dressed in tweeds and brogues and sensible grey lisle stockings. She taught French, speaking out of the side of her mouth with the exaggerated 'BBC' accent affected by those who follow hounds on foot and know someone who rowed for Oxford.

She introduced us to fencing, thereby opening a small side door into such lofty institutions as Battle Abbey and even Roedean, and there was a marked drop-out from Guides, Craft and Greek Dancing, all of us anxious to climb into white suits and face masks and shout 'En garde!' as we Erroll Flynn'd around the gym.

Topsy's formal aggression with the épée found a more primitive outlet in the field of punishment meted out to classroom offenders. Once, despatched to wait in the Science Lab for some misdemeanour, I was alarmed when at the end of class Topsy came storming down the stairs, flung open the door to the lab and stood staring at me, hands on hips, bosom heaving.

'By God!' she exploded. 'If I were a man I'd take you into the gym and KNOCK YOU DOWN!'

There was no answer to that, not when you are fourteen and, more particularly, when the rest of your class, convulsed with mirth, is standing on the Domestic Science lab table next door, peering through the glass partition waiting for the blood to flow. For Topsy it was a pyrrhic victory, for her threat to 'take you into the gym and knock you down' became public property, a screamingly funny joke which she could never stamp out without admitting to her colleagues that she was the author.

But, as with all rules, there are always exceptions, and here is a splendid one.

'By God!' she exploded. 'If I were a man I'd take you into the gym and knock you down!'

Mademoiselle, 'Mammy', the third pillar of the staff, was ageless, dishevelled, with white hair and a snarl which could turn one to stone or a smile as good as Chevalier's. She had authority, one obeyed her. Her stomach rolled out to support her bust; she shuffled along balanced precariously as a pair of scales between two carrier bags, overflowing with corrected exercise books. She was fierce, she was sweet. We hated her, we loved her. During her years at the school she must have paced every classroom from end to end leading pupils in recitals of 'La Fontaine' a million times. But heavens, will I ever forget . . .

> *Monsieur Corbeau, sur un arbre perché, tenait dans*
> *son bec un fromage . . .*

She got us through our exams, she drummed into us French with an energy that was unsurpassed in any other subject.

There follows a very varied and comprehensive survey of teachers of the past – liked, disliked, dull, amusing, good, bad, dreaded, worshipped – that will equally discourage and encourage those planning a scholastic career.

—An off-beat teacher was the science mistress, known as 'Jerks' (her name was Joachim). One holiday she took four of us to see *The Immortal Hour* at a small theatre in Euston. The following term, we four were together in a bedroom in the annexe, Oakleigh. Jerks had a room there too.

   She had large brown eyes and long black hair and she came to us one night, carrying a candle, with her dark hair flowing. She sat on a bed and very quietly sang 'How beautiful they are the lordly ones.'

   She was no beauty but she could conjure it up for others.

—Looking back, I can feel every sympathy with those poor young women, in their first job, which must have been so important for them. They all had university degrees – a matter of pride for the school. But they often came from very poor homes, and were learning how to teach (under supervision), probably for little more than their 'Keep'. Their accommodation was worse than ours, in dormitories under the roof, beside the servants' quarters. They ate the same meals as we did and watched hungrily, as we did, when the senior mistresses had their little extra tit-bits served. They supervised our once-a-week hot baths and escorted us on our daily walks in crocodile. We, little horrors that we were, despised their shabbiness and frowstiness.

—The nuns were 'ladies' in the old-fashioned meaning of the term, many from old Catholic landed families, and for the most part, charming educated women, with many interesting links in Britain and the continent. It was their link with the continent that I found so useful afterwards, as the order had finishing schools in Paris, Fribourg, and Rome, as well as London. To Paris, Rome, Fribourg and Salzburg I went in due course on very advantageous terms as pupil teacher/chaperone.

As the nuns entered the convent when young, many of them retained the expressions current at those times, hence they would say 'Ripping' or 'Topping', but they maintained far too many links with the outside world ever to lapse into infantilism as one finds in some orders, or the odd highly charged expressions or ardent affection for Christ or the Blessed Virgin, that would make one uncomfortable.

Their message was unsentimental; loyalty, integrity, honour, self-abnegation, self-control, and constant thought for others. Our singing of the Holy Week Ritual gave me a taste for fine church music, and I had a strong historical sense of the figures in church history . . .

—The English teacher was much feared; she used to call us by our surnames as though we were boys and during lessons would hurl our composition books back at us with a curl of the lip and a sarcastic remark, while the poor girls sitting next to her in the dining-room were always expected to provide non-stop witty and entertaining conversation. I always made a supreme effort to be first at her table on a Tuesday in order to pick the right seat which would take me round next to her on her day off! She had a cat called Julius Caesar who sat on her shoulder as she walked round the school and, for the cat's birthday, she went into a local bakery and ordered a cake on which the words 'Happy Birthday Julius Caesar' were to be written!

—Another mistress I recall with deep affection was a small gentle art mistress, one of three spinster sisters. Her name was Maud Huntsman and I called her 'Hunt-a-Rabbit'. She was always saying, 'You mustn't call me "Hunt-a-Rabbit", at least, not in class, dear!'

She couldn't keep order and we all behaved disgracefully. But we were shamed when P.M.L. came in and found most of us larking about under the trestle tables and the carefully arranged flowers ignored. After that it wasn't 'done' to rag poor Hunt-a-Rabbit and some of us even found we enjoyed art.

One winter holiday I stayed for a week with the three sisters, in their little house on the edge of a common. It was a week of delights. Magic lantern show in the village hall, Church bazaar, carol singing. I won a bottle of lavender water and some popcorn (yes, I'm sure it *was* popcorn!) and I was shown off to Hunt-a-Rabbit's friends. I didn't deserve such spoiling.

—In the early days, mistresses slept in the house and were present at all meals but later we had the two staff houses and maids lived in them too. The staff were then able to have a much more peaceful existence and only the Heads of the Lodge and Little St John's, with Matrons, were resident. The teachers were on duty for walks, games and on Sundays, for Church etc. The younger girls especially were always supervised, and this of course meant many hours altogether which are spared in most schools now. The most trying custom was to supply a chaperone for the music master. For many years he was an elderly man with a bald head and very gentle disposition. When at last I told him that I thought we could dispense with the chaperone, he said, 'I will, of course, tell you at once if I have any cause for complaint!' It would have been a very thankless task to try and start a romance in that direction.

It was this master who composed both words and music for our School Song, but in such a high key that it could not arouse great enthusiasm:

On Bexhill's western slopes there stands St John's so tall and stately,
By many hearts in many lands 'tis loved and treasured greatly, etc . . .

—The greatest staff at the college in my day was M. J. Chorlton, and there is no disguising her name for no tribute to her can ever be sufficiently far-flung, and I had the wonderful good fortune to be under her sway for the whole of my first year. She was of that great breed of born form mistresses whose instinctive combination of teaching and characterguiding amounted to genius. Sandy-haired and spectacled, with a gentle but astringent sarcasm, she would gaze upon her fascinated form sometimes with alert speculation, sometimes with far-away dreaminess, and in either case would allow a fine white handkerchief constantly to glide through the fingers of her exquisite hands; this had a mesmeric effect upon her young hopefuls and lulled them into an imprudent state of repose. Then she would pounce, but so endearing was her irony that even the victim could not forbear to smile with the rest.

Once, having a bad cold, I lost my voice and Matron sent me to bed. On my way upstairs I went and stood by Chorley's desk and mouthed at her in impotent silence.

'What on earth's the matter with you, child?' she asked, and then as I still mopped and mowed soundlessly, '*Don't* tell me you've lost your voice? Heaven be praised, child, we shall have some peace at last. Go to bed.'

None of us realised how closely Chorley watched over us, assessed our pros and cons, and deeply and sincerely prayed for us. Her therapy was always original, and one night she wandered into my room on Top Storey where I was at that stage of getting ready for bed of being off with the old and not yet on with the new.

'Just go on washing, dear, and don't pay any attention to me,' she said, sitting down on the bed and settling herself comfortably. 'We're all made the same, my dear . . . all made the same . . .' and then, practically without a pause:

'Tell me, Barbara, *why* are you so naughty?' and I gave her the answer which, she told me in after years, took the wind more completely out of her sails than any other she ever received.

'Because I'm so *happy* here, Miss Chorlton,' I said, breathless with the release of a heart's burden.

'Aren't you happy at home?'

'No, Miss Chorlton . . . My people don't get on.'

'H'mph!' said Chorley.

—Nethy (Mother Nethertine) terrorised us. We could always tell ahead when one of her bombshells was on the way. She would make the grand entrance into her classroom, lips pursed, face white and silent; then, seated at her high desk on the dais, she would lift up ber brass bell in the shape of a crinolined lady and ring it once, little finger extended, while we quaked waiting for the vitriol aimed at one of us, usually me!

Once I was arranging the statue of the Sacred Heart preparing for her feast day 6th June, and I broke it. She made me feel like a criminal; with tears in her eyes she said old Rev. Mother had given it to her. For weeks she collected 3d a week from me to buy a new one at Fr. V. H.'s repository. As I only had 5s a term it was tough going.

—One of them told us that she and another young teacher had gone to the Head with much trepidation to ask for an advance on their salaries which were then, at least, paid at the end of every term. Apparently the Head agreed instantly, adding 'Thank heavens for that. I thought you were both pregnant.' This, since one was single and the other divorced, did not go down too well.

One of the house underlings was, however, called 'Butch' by her superior in unguarded moments and had an effective method of getting us up in the morning by putting a cold and bony hand down the bed, which even then caused comment – and early rising.

—Our nuns were shrouded from top to toe in deepest black, counterpointed by a small fiercely starched area of white linen from which a face peered with a variety of expression. Our nuns were purposeful, firm, not woolly-headed liberals in any way. Two of them whom I remember especially could have shown the SAS how to do it – both veering round the six feet mark, of firm tread and able to cover the ground walking at speeds surpassing our childish running.

There was Mother Frances with a ramrod back and loping gait who struck terror whenever she appeared; her voice had the volume and carrying power of a pre-war Isolde. She stood no nonsense. In support there was Mother Gertrude, who moved on silent feet lightly, like Mohammed Ali in his prime. Whenever one was perpetrating any naughtiness there she was (as is her Master . . . omnipresent) looming over the miscreant. Her face was immensely solemn, rather ruddy skinned, but she had the most marvellous Cheshire cat grin, which the senior girls were sometimes privileged to see.

—In fact we were all very fond of our house mistress, Miss Spinks, known of course as Spinko. She was very old, we thought (all of fifty, I suppose), wore long dresses, which were very dated and she had a little dog. We had great respect for her and did not like to displease her. She was an absolute saint to my mother when my sister was very ill and my mother never forgot this.

—I remember many teachers of this era with respect and affection. I recall an incident with Miss Parsons who showed great humour and dignity. Newly arrived at Riddlesworth as our English teacher, she always started lessons with, 'Hi, Ladies!' Once in a grammar lesson, I noticed that she intoned: 'Lucy Lorket lorst her porket,' so I wrote this down in my jotter and passed it to my neighbour, but the offending pad was confiscated. Never apparently glancing at my rude scribblings, Miss Parsons continued with the lesson and let me collect the jotter, but I found written in her handwriting – 'and she lorst her jorter too!'

—We were not allowed by one nun to say Middlesex. We were expected to say 'Middle-essex'. When saying the former, we tended to emphasise the last syllable, which, while we had absolutely no idea why, being girls of the purest dispositions, brought an air of intense embarrassment to that particular nun.

The teaching of music and elocution, both of them subjects that should be entirely pleasurable, brought problems.

—Every girl had to learn a musical instrument, usually starting with the piano. The ones who showed musical ability progressed to other instruments. The ones, like me, with no musical ability found the whole experience a calamity.

There were several music teachers but it befell my fate to be instructed by a positive dragon. On Sunday, after Chapel, the times of the dreaded lessons would be pinned up on the notice board and this date and time would hang heavily on my heart. I would approach the lesson with fear and trepidation and frequently would have my fingers banged so hard on the keys that my bitten nails would start to bleed.

Actually the blood was a life-saver because I would be told to stop and wipe the keys with spit and a duster and the torture would come to an end. Then to fill the allotted twenty minutes, my teacher would push me flying off the stool and say 'This is what it *should* sound like.'

As I picked myself up and stood trembling beside her she would miraculously transform from a fearsom dragon to an almost normal person as her nimble fingers whizzed up and down the keyboard making such wonderful music. It always amazed me that someone so terrifying and ferocious could produce such marvellous sounds.

Obviously, because she was so talented, my inept clumsiness made her even more frustrated and enraged. Eventually my mother did intervene on my behalf and although this was strongly frowned upon, her intervention did spare me from piano lessons for the last year of my school life. For this I was eternally grateful, but, ironically, I am eternally grateful that I *did* learn the piano too.

—So several times a week I was instructed by a large firm lady with a booming voice to say what sounded to me like The Ket Set on the Met – but the Carf ran up the Parf in a minute and a harf. (Years later I heard an Indian ask a conductor on a bus to be put down at the Pluff in Sluff – and I was right back with my elocution lessons.) I tried hard to please, but I couldn't really see why the Ket was better than the Cat. Luckily I already knew about of'en and orff – if ever they should crop up. Soon I was booming away with the best – Come butter come, Come butter Come, Mary waits at the Gate waiting for her buttered Cake, Come butter come. Though still a few problems with clouds and houses.

Most of the reminiscences take for granted in schools the presence of a satisfactory and complete domestic staff and indeed prior to 1939, housemaids, cooks, parlour maids and odd-job men were in plentiful supply, as were gardeners and groundsmen. Present-day Headmistresses, for whom the domestic side is often as much of a worry and preoccupation as the scholastic, may well be envious.

—Another custom which came down the generations was that we all made our beds on Sunday. One of the great-aunts happened to arrive on Saturday on a visit to a country house and on Sunday morning, when she went up to her room after breakfast, she heard one maid say to another, 'She is no lady, she has made her own bed.' If that is the definition of a lady, there cannot be many left in England today. It was not till the middle of the 1914–18 War that it became the custom for schoolgirls to make their own beds. In my own schooldays housemaids thought nothing of looking after the bedrooms which housed quite thirty girls and making all those beds, and after that, they sat down in the afternoon to do the mending. £16 per annum was considered a good wage for a housemaid, and, when they were allowed out in the afternoon, they had to be in at six o'clock.

—I am afraid that my method of engaging new maids in the good old days when there was a vacancy would be useless now. I never applied to a registry office but just put a notice on the kitchen door: 'Ten shillings reward for a new Kitchenmaid' (or Housemaid) and there was no further trouble. Someone always brought a friend.

—I count among my best friends a great many of those who served in the school during my pilgrimage in it. When the numbers in St John's grew to one hundred and twenty, we always had twenty maids and at one time, three years went by without a single change on the staff and quite a number had twenty years to their credit. Hilda Mary surpassed them all with twenty-one years. She came as a very young between-maid and ended up as cook in the Junior House. Soon after her arrival it was found necessary for her to part with all her teeth and have a false set. Those were the days before National Health Insurance and the school could not undertake to supply teeth all round. We finally decided to look out all our 'white elephants' and organize an auction sale. It was a great success as well as great fun and, as a result, Hilda Mary was able to choose a superb set of teeth.

—One morning the housekeeper in the Staff House phoned up to say that one of the maids had had a baby in the night. She had disturbed nobody and you will hardly believe that the Head of the Junior House where she worked, had noticed nothing though she herself was one of a family of thirteen. The hospital nurse and the Matron had been equally unobservant. This emergency necessitated an inquest, which I attended, and also a good deal of planning for the future of the maid.

—Naturally, among so many, they were not all angels. One cook who came daily, had an unusually large crown to her hat and we often joked about it till we discovered that it went home every day full of meat pâtés and other oddments! A charlady, also daily, did not turn up one morning and the Chief of Police phoned to report that she had been arrested and to ask me if I should like to view her takings in case I wished to claim anything. I found a room filled with an endless variety of goods, including dining room chairs, curtains, silver, cutlery, etc. She had broken into houses at night when people were away. There was nothing of mine but a few days later I received a letter from the woman from Holloway prison asking me to write to the judge and say that she had stolen nothing from me. In view of what I had seen, it seemed unnecessary . . .

The maids usually gave amazingly little trouble. At one time we noticed that a bell was rung every morning to summon the housemaids from upstairs and I realized that this coincided with the arrival of a very good-looking butcher boy. After some time had been wasted, I rang up the butcher and asked if he could substitute a less handsome messenger. He was glad to know why many customers had complained of the late arrival of their joints. Nothing was said in the kitchen, but thenceforward a very plain and spotty youth appeared instead of an Adonis and the call bell was silent.

It was the same butcher who told me how much he and his wife enjoyed sitting on the parade on Sundays and watching our 'crocodile' go by. I was expecting him to make some compliment on the beauty of the girls but he added 'And I say to her "there goes our good meat . . ." '

—There was very little illness among the maids but, if anyone was ever absent, the others quickly filled the gap and made no difficulties. They were always ready to help each other and in one case this led to disaster. A between-maid had just been promoted to wait in the dining-room and as she hurried out to fetch a colossal rice pudding, the kitchen-maid helpfully advanced to the door with it. Alas! The two collided and poor Joan received the pudding all over her face. Luckily Sister was handy and applied tea, so the burns left no mark, but the maid was away for a fortnight getting well, and it must have been agony for her.

—There was a wonderful man called Moran, a huge Irishman who lived in the lodge and did all the odd jobs about the school. He was responsible for the boilers and the drains and cleaning all our shoes, taking out the Principal's dog last thing, posting letters to catch the 9.00 p.m. collection, for taking our trunks up to the dormitories and down again for storage, when we had unpacked and was at everyone's beck and call; he certainly belonged to no union.

—There was a boiler man, usually they had old chaps who were slightly dotty, but one term we found a young blond one (slightly dotty, nevertheless) whom we called Gloria, and who was in the habit of flexing his muscles at the older girls. His stay was brief, we didn't know why (but presumably somebody did).

—Among the men, the two of longest standing were
Dennett the chauffeur and Carley the handyman.
Quite a number of others earned a gold watch for
ten years' service and one of them married Hilda
Message. Dennett showed the cinema and the magic
lantern and also took charge of the filtration plant
for the swimming bath as well as the two cars, which
he kept perfectly. For eighteen years he was always
at hand for any emergency and I still miss his 'Just
as you think, Miss.' There was one very historic
occasion when he waited to let a very important
funeral procession pass. I asked Dennett if he
thought that the town would turn out like that for
my funeral. 'Certainly, Miss, if you have it on a
Wednesday!' (early closing day) was the prompt
reply.

4

Clothes

A minor benefit, and there are precious few of them, that the last war conferred on schools was a reduction, brought about by rationing, in those seemingly endless lists of school clothing required. One such list, appalling in its excessive demands (and why on earth twenty-four handkerchiefs?) has survived from the early 1930s.

    3 vests, 3 liberty bodices or
      Combinations
    6 pairs white knicker linings
    6 pairs navy blue knickers (elasticated)
    6 pairs socks, or stockings if over thirteen
    3 cotton dresses (summer)
    1 coat and skirt (tweed)
    1 gym tunic
    4 Viyella blouses
    1 tussore dress (summer)
    1 velveteen dress (winter)
    2 pairs walking shoes
    2 pairs house shoes
    1 pair galoshes
    1 pair gym shoes
    1 pair games shoes
    1 pair Wellington boots
   24 white cotton handkerchiefs

1 sweater
1 overcoat
1 blazer
1 macintosh and sou'wester
1 hat or beret
1 house tie
1 school tie
1 hat band
3 jumpers
2 skirts
1 garden hat (grey felt)
1 garden coat
Gloves, scarf, brush and comb
1 rug
1 eiderdown
Sheets, towels
1 Bible, 1 Prayer book
1 workbasket

Many will remember how every one of these items had to be packed and taken home, after being duly ticked off on the list, at term's end and then brought back again at the beginning of each term. Hence those vast trunks manhandled by porters, that vanished breed, at Waterloo and Paddington. No garment, however unwanted at home, could ever be left at school, biding its time.

However, in at least one case the acquiring of new, school clothes was no by means unpopular.

The clothes list sent me into raptures, though goodness knows it was dull enough. 'Two navy blue serge coats and skirts, 4 white flannel blouses, 2 silk blouses for Sunday, 1 black velour hat, 1 overcoat.' There was no time to be lost. Mother and I bade farewell to kind Mrs Trimble and hurried up to London where we stayed at the same dull hotel in Notting Hill Gate. Why we felt this very ordinary outfit had to be bought in London I have no idea, but we did, and that was that.

We then went shopping and proceeded to make more mistakes over what we bought than you would believe possible. The trouble was the clothing list was specific, but not specific enough. We did all right with the blue serge coats and skirts – one thick and hairy for everyday and one thinner and smoother for Sundays, and we bought the right sort of flannel blouses. But we came badly unstuck over the silk blouses, which Mother bought with large, frilly, lace-trimmed collars to look a bit dressy for Sundays, but which only resulted in me being christened 'Little Lord Fauntleroy' by amused classmates in severely tailored shirts. Then the overcoat; the list certainly said navy blue, but Rita had a perfectly good outgrown coat which fitted me, only it was mauve. I wept, I begged, but it was no good. The mauve coat I had to wear, and that branded me from the start. Mauve is definitely not my colour but Mother seems to have been addicted to it because she bought me a mauve artificial silk dress for evenings, and if you don't know what artificial silk was in those early days of manmade fibres then you have missed nothing. It was terrible.

The next mistake we made was with the stockings. 'Four prs. woollen stockings' said the list. Now, I had always worn black, but feeling that all life was changing and that my legs might as well change with it, I plumped for brown. Wrong. Everyone else wore black. Jessie and I dyed those stockings in a bowl over the nursery gas ring the first holidays I spent at Minchinhampton, and managed to spill the dye all down the nursery wall, which the small cousins enjoyed and Auntie Stella did not.

A Suffolk-reared correspondent gives an extremely comprehensive picture of what the average 1930s' schoolgirl wore and looked like at different seasons, times of day, and days of the week.

Whenever a new item of uniform is introduced, it is greeted with great enthusiasm by the girls but, as soon as the novelty wears off, the new is execrated along with the old. Whether or not the pupils of Felixstowe had good reason to complain in the 1930s, their parents certainly had, for the very lengthy uniform lists must have taken some paying for. Quite apart from the really expensive items like coats and dresses, numerous pairs of shoes were required for different occasions, including galoshes. Black silk stockings were *de rigueur* on Sundays and the list enumerated camisoles, combinations and liberty bodices.

Starting with Sunday best, Miss Nineteen-Thirties wore a matching dress and coat in black and white checks and a black (later grey) velour hat with a red band, inherited from the old Uplands School. When the school went into mourning for King George V, the red band was changed to black. It was unfortunate that these checked garments bore a certain resemblance, being rather square as well as black and white, to washbags sold everywhere in a well-known chain store. Rude boys from other schools in Felixstowe were known to shout 'Woolworth sponge-bags' at our miserably embarrassed girls as they took their Sunday stroll along the Promenade. The outfit was completed by leather gloves and a stiff rust-coloured scarf – completely devoid of any warmth but worn as a cravat – and naturally, flat black laced shoes. On weekdays, happily, the 'sponge-bag' was discarded in favour of a grey Harris tweed coat with a half-belt at the back and the headgear was a red beret, worn as far to the back of the head as possible. The beret had a tiny stalk at the top but as soon as a new girl arrived, some old hand would instruct her in how to snip it off – nobody could be seen with this little tuft proclaiming her newness!

During the week, instead of the Sunday dress, one wore a long-sleeved cream blouse and house tie, either with a grey skirt or a box-pleated tunic and red girdle. On cold days, a grey V-necked jumper with a red band was added. When it was too warm for a coat, a red blazer, still one of the smartest items of College uniform, could be worn. Particularly hated were the thick, tickly grey woollen stockings which had to be worn during the day. Once again, the reminiscences of Old Girls are invaluable. 'We had a grey games hat called a Pork Pie which we wore jauntily squashed in and at a rakish angle on the back of the head, leaving a page-boy hairdo or plaits nicely exposed. It was never, in our eyes, to keep our heads warm! There was also a white long-sleeved pullover with a wine-coloured stripe at the neck. We draped this over our shoulders. I never remembered wearing it, it was a sort of adornment.'

After games there was a chilly 'strip-wash' in the dormitories and everyone changed into evening uniform. This was a long-sleeved grey marocain dress with a white detachable collar and a narrow red ribbon tied at the neck in a bow. There were no nylons or tights in those days but it must have been a relief to take off the itchy woollen stockings and put on grey lisle, even if these were pretty thick. The dress had to be protected from inky prep. until supper-time so it was covered with a red-and-white checked overall. The heavy laced shoes were changed for black strapped ones. One Old Girl recalls that she had two pairs of each and that one's school number was marked on the instep with nails. However, with evening uniform, Sixth and Upper Fifth – oh joy! oh rapture! – could wear court shoes with HEELS! These were envied, admired, remarked on and much sought after by the lower orders, who waited for years for the pleasure of putting on these delectable items, only to be so self-conscious when the great day of liberation dawned, that they scarcely had the courage to run the gauntlet of criticism shown in all eyes – staff and girls – and perhaps put off the launching until the next evening.

The Sunday dress had the same white collar and red ribbon as the weekday dress and, similarly, had to be covered up safely with the red-and-white overall, only to be revealed for church, for lunch and supper and for going out with parents.

The summer uniform was not too bad – a red-and-white cotton dress for daytime, worn with the handsome red blazer. For games, the girls wore what was probably their favourite garment known as a 'djibbah'. It was made of heavy pale grey linen and was very comfortable. Although it looked shapeless, it was cinched at the waist with a red girdle, or 'colours' if one belonged to a team. It had a Peter Pan collar and two large pleats at the sides to allow for lungeing at tennis or grabbing for that masterly catch in cricket. Those who were rabbits at cricket were sent out to 'deep' where they made daisy chains and earned 'Should try harder' on their summer reports.

If the 'djibbah' was the favourite, undoubtedly the summer Sunday uniform was the one most disliked – cream tussore dress with red bow and short sleeves, matching tussore coat, very square and very, very expensive. Rumour has it that this outfit disappeared suddenly from the uniform list after a parent received it back from the laundry during the holidays, labelled 'Gentleman's large dressing-gown'.

One hesitates to raise a distasteful subject but facts are facts and must be faced, here the subject being olfactory emanations (smells).

As for ourselves, we cannot have been much better – we had a limit for the number of garments allowed in our weekly laundry – one nightdress, one pair of combinations, one pair of knickers, one pair of brown woollen stockings, and handkerchiefs. Girls who had reached menstruation were allowed a dozen of those awful linen diapers, as extras.

Our uniform was really very striking, but impractical. We had a pretty, green serge long-sleeved dress, green serge bloomers, a lovely, scarlet, silk sash and flowing tie and green hair ribbons. On walks we wore heavy woollen scarlet cloaks, with peaked hoods and in winter green golf jackets; with straw boaters in the summer with a green red-bordered band and shield, embroidered with our motto 'Truthe Shalle Delivere'. (The Head's father had been a professor of Anglo Saxon.) Thick brown woollen stockings completed our weekday uniform. We wore dresses of our own choice on Sunday and, in the summer, shantung coats and our own pretty hats. Our serge dresses went to be dry cleaned during the holidays, but for girls at an age when their glands were working overtime, and who had only one hot bath per week, and with our hair washing limited to once a month, we must have smelt pretty awful! I know our poor little junior mistresses were frequently the subject of cruel comment at times! Of course our icy swill each morning was called a 'cold bath', but on a sub-zero dawn, few of us washed efficiently.

And more along the same lines.

We had one everyday serge blue winter dress, worn for twelve to thirteen weeks at a time and then mercifully dry-cleaned. In order to look spruce we had white collars attached by press-studs. We were not allowed to call them 'poppers' as this was childish. These collars were re-allocated twice per week and we spent hours of finger-pricking needlework keeping the ghastly ten press-studs on collar and dress intact. This managed to combat the dirty-neck syndrome, but what of the smelly armpits?

Well, a cunning device called a dress shield was inserted into the dress, again by press-studs. There were four pairs of studs to each shield making a total of twenty-six fiendish little silver demons that had to be sewn and re-sewn into the drab blue serge to make it struggle through the two winter terms. In view of the fact that lustful deodorants were banned, the easily laundered dress shields were essential.

In the summer term we had a clean royal blue cotton dress *every* week without dress shields and so in a heat wave (as there so often used to be when one was young) the dresses were pretty niffy by the end of the week. We were also allocated with one pair of navy blue knickers for the week – enough said!

Here a Headmistress speaks up strongly both for the virtues of conformity and the splendidly durable toughness of the ordinary gym tunic.

Our girls wore gym tunics all day till they changed before tea. I was amazed that some parents complained that those much-tried gym tunics did not last more than two years. I fully agreed with the makers that their endurance was quite amazing. Those who have always been accustomed to uniform cannot realize what a blessing it is. Parents know exactly what to get and there is no fear of competition making things miserable for the less wealthy children. The general appearance of the school is also much smarter.

Every child hates to be different from the rest if any uniformity of clothes or behaviour is expected. Girls have often told me of cases when a mother has insisted

that something must 'make do' and it has been absolute
agony. One girl with a figure like a plank wrote home
and asked her mother to send a 'bust bodice' – not to
wear, but just to possess, as other girls had them.

A maiden aunt was exceedingly kind to a niece, who
was also her godchild. She paid her school fees as well
as all the expenses of her journey home from abroad
and all her holidays and her outfit, but one grievous
mistake spoilt it all. She sent the niece to a school with
a discarded dressing-gown of her own generation. I
can see it now, hanging on the door and the child's
face looking at it.

A middle-aged colonel told me lately that he will
never forget the ignominy of winning a race at his prep.
school, in grey running shoes which should have been
white. Parents should never make children feel con-
spicuous if it can possibly be helped. It is futile to say
that they ought not to mind. They do.

Oddly enough, gym tunics were not always used for gym.

—The clothes list for returning to school was as immu-
table as the Law of the Medes and Persians. One
article in particular has remained clearly in my
memory – this was (or these were) knicker linings –
large white cotton garments, in shape like the long
khaki shorts worn by sporty young men of the day.
They were made by Mother, cut out on our sitting-
room floor; we wore them 'next to us', underneath
the navy blue bloomers (elastic at waist and leg).
We were thus very bulky maidens, the effect being
enhanced by the peacock blue (our school colour)
panelled tunics – which did not suit every figure.

While on the subject of clothing – for gym class,
we removed the tunic, kept on our blouses and ties,
and tucked the blouses into the top of the bloomers,
with the result that those of us *not* of athletic aspirations, resembled jesters of the medieval period of

history, with the thick black woollen hosen, and sturdy plimsolls to round them off. Strangely, those girls who lived for gym and hockey seemed to be bouncy and keen enough to slough off the strange effect of their garb, while they nimbly climbed ropes, or leapt over the horse like feathers – but we poor souls, who hated gym, hung miserably in line waiting our turn and hoping that, just once, we might not be seen . . . Talking of climbing ropes: I never got off the knot in all the years I was there. Strongly though my hands (chilblained) swarmed up the rope, the rest of me never followed . . .

—It was no longer the custom to shower the Head-mistress with rose petals on her birthday, but Greek dancing, for example, was still on the curriculum. For this we were robed in pale blue tunics made of some vile synthetic fabric (called, probably, something like Celanese or Nutex), totally unflattering, in which we had to imagine ourselves wood nymphs, daffodils, etc. (None of which, incidentally, was ever related to the Greeks in any way.) The odd part of this was the dancing teacher herself, who looked and dressed like nothing so much as the ageing Madame of a Blackpool brothel, although she was a fearful snob and did in fact have the appropriate accents and, apparently, connections.

School uniforms vary considerably and the following choice of term-time rig seems to me especially colourful and charming.

The uniform was a mid-brown Harris Tweed suit and matching coat, with dark brown felt hat and leather gloves (straw and peach cotton in summer). Blouses were pale pink Vyella and worn with either a beige cardigan or dark brown jumper. Stockings were 60-denier Aristoc Peach petal. Summer dresses were blue and white striped cotton with a bias-cut skirt. Evening

Strongly though my hands (chilblained) swarmed up the rope, the rest of me never followed . . .

wear – theatres etc. – was a full-skirted needle-cord dress in either blue, red or green. Games kit was a yellow wool jumper, yellow Aertex shirt and brown gaberdine games skirt/culotte, with dark green track-suit for hockey. Dance was performed (or not) in a shapeless blue tunic. The most useful item of uniform was a voluminous brown wool hooded cape, the unceremonious jumbling of which I have frequently regretted. Vests and liberty bodices were on the list (although I don't recall ever owning the latter), 'brass-ieres, if worn'. The regulation knicker was dark brown and voluminous and to be worn with 'white cotton lining'. Both had exceptionally good elastic and would doubtless have thwarted all but the most determined onslaught. We were also allowed to wear our own clothes – 'mufti' – in the evening but not, I think, on Sunday.

Elsewhere there was a sad reluctance to move with the times.

Our uniform was traditional from the time the school was founded. We wore green serge dresses with sailor collars and dickies and belts all trimmed with a double row of gold braid. These were known as 'callies'; we wore them for lessons and for games winter and sum-mer and they were most unhygienic. Callisthenics were exercises for cultivating gracefulness and strength and taught in girls' schools before drill, gym, PT or, as now, PE. Several years after I started we were allowed to wear green cotton dresses in the summer and they were at least washable. All dresses had to touch the ground when kneeling and one summer evening four of us tucked up our callies and played leapfrog in the garden and ran away from the mistress on duty. The awful punishment was that we had to wear our serge winter callies for a fortnight and stand out in front at Prayers.

After games we changed into blouses and skirts for

tea; on Sundays we had navy blue satin blouses, but in the summer white blouses, white coats and skirts and terrible straw hats with wide white ribbon threaded through the straw and a large bow at the side. When our Royal President died the whole school went to church in white costumes with black mourning bands on our arms. On Saturdays we changed into white dresses, but short sleeves or low necks were not allowed; after supper there was ballroom dancing in the big hall. When white dresses went out of fashion we had old-gold shantung dresses supplied by Liberty; these were supposed to tone with the oak panelling and were very pretty. Brown shoes and stockings were worn out of doors and black indoors, so that no one could stay in wet stockings and catch a cold. No stockings were worn for games and some people found that very cold and miserable. The only break from uniform was that we were allowed to wear any jerseys or cardigans we liked and this certainly cheered things up; they were referred to as knitted blouses by the Principal.

It was natural for the more clothes-conscious girls to resent wartime rationing.

Dress was a very sore point with those of us whose teenage schooldays took place during the war, and we deeply resented spending precious clothes coupons on the school uniform. We had an eye for 'glamour' – after all we'd been getting regular doses of Hollywood movies ever since we were tinies in the 1930s. My ideal was the satin-and-slinky-cut-on-the-cross splendour of Carole Lombard, Myrna Loy and Jean Harlow, but at school, of course, we wore baggy navy knickers, rumply lisle stockings and saggy, shiny serge (one gymslip had to last me for about four years, with discreet letting down and out). Hopefully, however, in the early 1940s we tried to evoke Veronica Lake's peek-a-boo-bang in our hairstyles, which at least were not affected by rationing. I am sure that by no stretch of the imagination could we ever have resembled her, but this was our one attempt at glamour in school uniform. The authorities demanded that all coiffures should be tied back, if the hair were long enough to touch our shoulders, so constant battles raged over this between 'us' and 'them'. We were scrubbed in public if our faces bore traces of lipstick or powder, and warned about expulsion should the offence be repeated. If caught outside the school precincts minus the regulation velour or panama hat, we were sentenced to wear it all day *in* school. (Ghastly humiliation!) And we were punished if discovered eating sweets in our uniforms in the streets or on buses. This rigid upholding of our standards of behaviour – reminiscent of Angela Brazil's formidable Headmistresses – continued throughout the war, contrasting strangely with the liberality of many of the school's attitudes. Clothes rationing allowed us little scope for experimentation in personal attire, and as a change from the navy blue gymslip and white blouses of our school uniform, padded-shouldered afternoon dresses and wedge-heeled shoes seemed the epitome of elegance. Pocket money was also severely rationed for me during my days at school and it was this, perhaps, as much as patriotic fervour that made me respond wholeheartedly to government exhortations to 'Make Do and Mend'. When I could get hold of my brother's old shirts I tore them up and made handkerchiefs from them, and in the holidays, to my great satisfaction, I found a way of improvising mascara with a damp, discarded toothbrush and my father's typewriter ribbon.

I was tolerably bright, and therefore destined to study French *and* Latin as well as my native language. So only one school year could be allocated from my timetable to the acquisition of sewing skills. (Soon after leaving I found that, in the circles *I* moved in, a sewing-machine, rather than a diamond, was a girl's best friend, and I had to make up for lost time in learning how to use one.) Now one hour a week for one year is not a large dollop of time; one year, of course, comprises three terms, and what happened at school was this. In Term One we had to make something to cover the desk, and to put our eventual sewing-work on. Whether we were supposed to be protecting the desk from the sewing or the sewing from the desk was never clarified! The desk cover was fawn (crash, I think the material was called) with a dull green edging that had to be stitched on and then embroidered in chain stitch with one's *full* name. As mine was Mary Rose Stephanie, my task was daunting indeed compared with that of, say, my form-mate Jane Evans, and I gnashed my teeth at the injustice of this.

In Term Two, with the desk covers triumphantly completed, we thought we might get down to business and make CLOTHES. But no! We first had to rustle up – guess what? – a bag to put our future sewing in. And – guess what again? – the bag was to be made of fawn crash, with a dull green drawstring through it, and it had to be embroidered in chain stitch with our *full* names etc . . . This took us the whole of the second term, sewing laboriously by hand.

Then Term Three arrived and we were told that now, yes, we really were considered ready and able to make something we could actually *wear*. Our joy, however, at this inspiriting news was short-lived; the sewing mistress had already decided exactly what we should each make, and this was a magyar nightie of such hideous material, monstrous shape and size that, though I took the whole term making it, I couldn't wait to get home and bung it on to the boiler.

No account of regulation school clothes would be complete

without a mention of the famous outfitters whose name will strike a chord with many.

Our school uniforms came from Daniel Neal's. Our Sunday dresses were a little different – in the winter we wore emerald green dresses (one of the school colours) and a black velour hat which was smaller than our weekday velour hats and had a matching emerald green hat band (to denote that we were boarders). In the summer on Sundays we wore white silk dresses, white gloves, black silk stockings, black patent leather strap shoes, and white panama hats with a small brim reminiscent of an upturned jerry, except that it had a green hatband on it. However, due to the school being at an extremely cold and exposed part of Kent and with such a freezing building, our underwear in the winter was really entrancing – first a Chilprufe vest with sleeves, then Chilprufe combinations, topped up with a liberty bodice, black woollen stockings and navy blue 'bloomers'. Make-up in those days was completely unheard of by us, also anything resembling a hair curler.

And so to hats . . .

I recall the uniform in some detail because it was pretty grim. Hats, summer Sundays, we wore 'Rosy Pearls'. These were wide-brimmed, cream-coloured coarse straw with a ring of very small pink roses round the crown, hence the name. These were worn with cream-coloured serge coats and skirts, *not* kind to budding female figures.

Weekday summer hats, white panama(?) with green ribbon, and, after school, quite pleasant green silky cotton dresses with white collars and cuffs.

Winter – Sunday hats – known as 'Cabbages'. Black velour with a wide band of emerald green ribbon, set off by a ghastly pleated green cockade, like an Irish rising sun.

These were worn with a fiendish navy blue 'coat frock'. This was a tube of serge which buttoned down the back (catching one's hair) and had a two-part white collar which needed frequent changing. It was sheer hell to get the two points of the collar in the exact centre.

Twiggy might have carried off the wearing of such a garment but there were few Twiggies and *we mostly resembled navy blue beer barrels*.

The afternoon winter dress was favourite. This had to be green velveteen, but choose your own style.

And so to footwear . . .

Then there were the footwear rituals. Despite wartime clothes shortages, we were supposed to have an extensive wardrobe of shoes. We had always to put on sturdy lace-ups for outdoors, even if we just popped across from one school building to another; these had to be changed for black buttoned glacé ones when we were indoors, except if we were heading for the horrors of the parallel bars and that fearfully long, frightfully hard, wooden horse we were expected to shin up and over in the gym; then grey canvas shoes, elasticated across the instep, were the order of the day. But, if the rain wasn't actually sheeting down, we might well be whisked out for rounders onto the playing fields, when black plimsolls had to be donned. Playing fields at girls' schools, though never acquiring the mystique of those associated with educational establishments for boys, nevertheless *can* boast their own legends. Across the vastness of ours, apparently, Henry VIII used once to court Anne Boleyn, on horseback, we were told proudly by the games mistress. What images this gave our adolescent minds to conjure with! Something that helped to while away those endless summer hours that one spent in cricket matches fielding on the boundary to which no-one, not even dear old Daisy Barker, captain and cricket whizz-kid, could send the ball. But back to shoes, it was the same black plimsolls for netball; hockey demanded the toughness of studded leather boots, and for cricket and tennis we had to wear white plimsolls.

We spent so much time in getting ready to do things that I suspected the Baden-Powells had over-sold the 'Be Prepared' idea to our Headmistress and staff. (The school had its own Guide company, but I gave this a wide berth.) We had to dash in and out of shorts (grey for gym and navy for games) and into overalls (blue and white gingham for dommy sci., green for art and fawn for 'stinks').

Time was when luckless housemaids, overworked and under-paid, had, in their limited spare time, to do all the mending. But no more.

Every Saturday morning we would be incarcerated in the Common Room with a pile of clean numbered clothes to mend. Every article had one's number on it. Names were irrelevant – everyone was known by a number. In the junior years there would be a liberty bodice amongst the pile. This had four buttons around the base and a string of buttons all up the front. The four base buttons would need replacing freqently as they were required to take the full strain and responsibility of the stringy suspenders.

The stockings were required to be well hoisted so as not to show crinkles in a standing position. However, since we spent a good deal of our time kneeling in prayer, the inevitable strain meant that something had to give and this was always the liberty bodice button. It usually flew off in Assembly during prayers and would leap from your leg and shoot across the hall to much stifled merriment and mirth from on-lookers.

Two pairs of bright brown lisle stockings were amongst the pile. The ladders appearing in these could be enormous. The holes had to be darned with intricate works of art with threads going in and out in weaving patterns. The ladders however were allowed to be 'cobbled'. This was a sort of frantic over-sewing from one end of the offending flash of daylight to the other, more often than not running from toe to top.

It was quite a relief when one's bust could no longer be forced into the lecherous liberty bodice. The suspender belt was never regarded as a sex-symbol like it is today. It was just another contraption with suspenders dangling from it to keep the beastly bright brown lisles well-hoisted.

The advent of brassiere-wearing was always a secret initiation ceremony with matron. From time to time, she would whisper an invitation to 'See me in the Linen Room' to about three or four big-breasted teenagers. There they would be thrust into pink (always pink) bosom-supporting undergarments and the days of the liberty bodice would be gone forever.

The vest, however, was never shed winter or summer. It was regarded in those days as having special medical properties. To have abandoned the wearing of it would have left yourself wide open to contracting polio, scarlet fever or diphtheria.

There has survived part of a clothing list compiled by 'Jane, aged nine', a list requiring explanations here and there.

> 1 Sholder Bag
> 1 tea shurt
> 1 cilt (kilt)
> pear of slipers
> 3 potows (photos)
> wash boy etc (wash bag)
> brush and comp
> dressing gown
> pea-jarmers (pyjamas)

5

Food

Memories of, and opinions about, school food vary considerably, especially as our recollections here cover two World Wars and the nutritional problems and privations that went with them. By and large, caterers and cooks come off fairly well and are appreciated rather more warmly than that modern scholastic invention, the Lady Dietician, with her obsession about calorific values and the importance of sprinkling almost everything in sight with grated carrot.

> Nobody ever worried about vitamins or any of the modern ideas as to nutrition at St John's in my time, or before it. We always had plenty of good food and it was always well-cooked and served. I can see now the large rounds of roast stuffed veal, which was our favourite meat course, but best of all were the sponge cakes and fruit. A very usual Saturday dinner was hot joint with roast potatoes and greens, followed by two oranges and two buns each, and everyone consumed them without turning a hair. People complain that children are greedy if they watch anxiously to see what is coming in at the door. Food is frightfully important when you are young and children are not usually greedy, but they like a lot.

Occasionally we come upon a resentful outburst.

School fare was a nasty shock to me. Pale yellow, tasteless cubes called scrambled egg, made from a synthetic powder. Enamel jugs of dark brown water called cocoa. Stews full of gristle and thick packet gravy. Rhubarb tarts whose pastry was like reinforced concrete. The Sunday treat with lumpy custard. The slabs of grey bread for tea were spread with army plum and apple jam in the morning, so that by tea time it had soaked through to the other side; my parents paid extra for me to have an apple to go to bed with, after 'Abide with me' had been sung over the congealing supper-plates.

But this particular food critic was soon to discover that it can be a mistake to speak out in public and that loyalty is expected in all matters.

When Half-Term came, with capital letters, my mother took me to lunch at one of Brighton's best and oldest restaurants, Muttons. I don't think it still exists. But its memory does in my mind. It was dark and crimson plushy. I had a mixed grill with my mother. She was rather horrified at the way I tucked in. I had never been a greedy child, quality meant more than quantity to me. 'If you saw the muck we're given at school, you wouldn't be surprised' I piped up, becoming eloquent over the poor quality of the quantities we were served at those long tables where we all moved up one place each week so that we each had our turn of sitting next to the presiding mistress or prefect with whom we had to make suitable conversation. Those at the bottom of the table could spread their slices of grey bread with mustard, pepper and salt, if they were hungry enough.

Half-term holiday was only one day back in the 1920s and a Sunday, so we didn't lose any work. On the Monday, after my blow-out at Mutton's, I was conducted by an icy prefect in a velvet snood and pigtail, the mark of the 'non-flighty' type of girl (the 'flighty' ones had bobbed hair and kiss-curls) to the sanctum of the three Miss Lawrences, the massive Triumvirate who ran the school. They sat in a row, their bunned hair shaded from grey to snow-white on the head of the Head, known as P.L., who was also the enormously fattest: she seemed carved into a sitting posture like a Buddha, but there was no half-smile. Her expression was grim as she began the indictment. I was not asked to sit down.

'A loyal old friend of the school has informed us that one of our girls, wearing the brown and navy hatband and tie of No. 2 House, was having lunch yesterday with her mother at Mutton's Restaurant. Were you there between one and two o'clock yesterday?' 'Yes.' 'You were heard speaking in a dreadful way about the school food. Is that true?' 'I described the food, which is dreadful, both in quality and in cooking of it.' 'Are you sorry for what you said?' I didn't answer. I gazed sullenly down at my feet in the large black strap shoes we had to wear indoors. 'You will not be immediately expelled. We shall allow you to stay until the end of term. We shall write to your parents to say that since you do not wish to conform to the spirit of the school, it is better if you do not return here after the holiday.' I tried to hide my delight at the sentence pronounced by P.L. I knew that my father would not approve of a school having spies reporting on what the girls said to their parents in restaurants, nor my mother either. And indeed, when the Triumvirate wrote to them in the holidays to say they had reconsidered their decision and hoped I would return in the Spring Term, they replied that they had already arranged to send me elsewhere. If this incident had occurred nowadays, I could probably have sued the school for snooping!

Eating and education went sometimes hand in hand.

Every term we each of us had to spend a week at Mademoiselle's table in the dining hall where only French was allowed to be spoken. Of course, if you were out of earshot of Mademoiselle it was rubbish French – 'Passez-moi les verts' and 'Ce poisson est un peu whiffy': things like that. Mademoiselle ate very little and we thought it was because she didn't like our English food, but a girl called Naomi invented a story that it was because she spent all her spare time in her bedroom guzzling tinned frogs' legs and snails and that she (Naomi) had seen her emptying snail shells with a clatter into the dustbin. Mademoiselle was really quite nice actually.

There was a terribly giggly girl called Averil – almost anything would set her off, you merely had to squint at her or roll your eyes and away she went. At the French table, if you were near Mademoiselle and talking to her, a funny thing to do was to say 'Oui' twice in succession and fairly quickly so that it came out sounding like 'Wee-wee, Mademoiselle', which must be different in French as Mademoiselle never twigged. Anyway, Averil was never proof against this and always collapsed totally. One day Miss Winters saw her giggling, and obviously at something wrong, and she sent her out of the room, followed her out and asked her why she was laughing. Averil lied like a trooper and we gave her part of our sweet ration for being so decent and protecting us.

In many cases, the school food was actually praised.

In spite of, or perhaps because of, the cold it must have been a healthy life because I developed an enormous appetite. There was no nonsense about slimming in those days. If you were fat you put up with it and just smiled a little wistfully when nicknamed Porky Boy after the famous character in *The Rainbow*. I was thin, and I ate like a horse. The food was one of the nice things about the school, it was really very good, though rather strange at times. Never since I left there have I had lentils for breakfast; not lentils on toast or curried, but just straight lentils. We loved them. Then there were beetroot fritters, known in the revolting parlance of the young as 'nosebleed fritters' and there were huge suet puddings smothered in chocolate sauce. The very idea of a combination of suet and chocolate makes me feel sick now, but it was one of our favourites.

It was only sensible to grab additional food items wherever and whenever they were legally obtainable.

The food was certainly adequate, but like all school children we were always hungry. So we supplemented our diet from our own grown radishes, hawthorn leaves and berries, sorrel, nasturtium leaves, orange peel etc. As was the usual custom when eating oranges, my sister solicited a crowd of girls thus engaged and asked each one for the peel, to which each one replied, 'Sorry, promised.' One Sunday afternoon when, as usual, I had been sent to bed in punishment, I was amusing myself stripped to the waist washing, with my hair screwed up on top in a garter like a sweep's brush, when a mistress suddenly dashed in saying, 'Come down to Assembly at once, something dreadful has happened.' 'I must dress first,' I protested, to which she replied, 'There is no time for that, come as you are, and *hurry*,' and with that she fled. Thinking the place must be on fire and the staircase falling in, I tore down just as I was to the astonishment and amusement of the whole school. The emergency was to *pray* for two girls who had eaten *Laburnum seeds* and were at that moment having their throats tickled with a feather by Sister in the San!

But to obtain an item illegally was unwise.

In my second term there was a tremendous sensation. It was quite soon after the last war and bananas were a great novelty and excitement, and a girl called Freda stole one from the kitchen and ate it in her dormitory and couldn't get rid of the skin, which Matron found next day in her handkerchief drawer. We all thought that Freda might be expelled, but instead of that the Head dreamt up a weird punishment. We were all summoned to the dining-room and Freda was made to sit at the staff table and every single member of the staff then ate a banana in front of Freda while glaring at her in disapproval. It put her off bananas for ever, which perhaps was the idea.

Some of the additional food items would hardly appeal to a gourmet stomach.

To supplement our 'meagre' fare, we would smuggle out of the refectory bread, which later we would make into sandwiches using, as a filling, condensed milk or Gibbs SR pink block toothpaste. Our navy-blue school knickers were an invaluable part of our uniform – the legs were elasticated and much could be carried inside without fear of it falling out in Chapel, or before it reached its destination. Any food we disliked intensely, or found completely unpalatable, we removed from the refectory in this manner. I know of one friend who, at her boarding school, had to eat Gibbs SR toothpaste sandwiches as a punishment!

Readers with sad memories of being made to eat brawn, whiskery bits and all, will be sympathetic to what follows and delighted by the highly ingenious solution to the problem.

Of the food I also remember little except for delicious breakfast porridge, and even more delicious golden syrup sandwiches for tea. These had been made hours in advance and were gloriously soggy with butter and

Bananas were great novelty after the last war . . . Freda stole one and ate it. She was made to watch as every staff member ate a banana in front of her, glaring at her in disapproval.

syrup. The breakfast porridge was frequently followed by brawn – a pink and brown mottled horror. Soon after my traumatic arrival at this establishment I developed what, in these more enlightened days, would be recognised as a psychosomatic disturbance. I was, on occasions, completely unable to swallow. The brawn produced this reaction, and I was always left sitting looking at it long after the other children had left the tables. Finally, in desperation my sister was called for to *make* me eat it. With the greater ingenuity of a nine-year-old she quickly saw that the brawn, chopped small, closely resembled the pink granite chips of the drive. We speedily emptied the lot through the open window on this and many subsequent occasions.

All schools rightly insisted on 'tidy plates' (everything gone down the red lane) and attempted to enforce this rule, not always with success.

My dormitory was called Guardian Angels – others had equally peculiar names, but at the tender age of ten, the worst aspect was the food – truly appalling, but served in sumptuous surroundings, damask tablecloths, serviettes – the lot! We had to eat *everything* and one memorable time, when Sister Agnes' porridge had really deteriorated, we all took to secreting it about our person in polythene bags for later disposal on dismissal from the refectory. Unfortunately, it does seem incredible, but the great majority of us disposed of it down the same three loos! It set like concrete – much to the amazement of the plumber.

Orderly processions were the required method of getting to the dining-room.

As the line proceeded downstairs to the dining-room, prefects were posted at various vantage points, known as cabstands, to make sure that nobody stepped out of line. The staff presided at breakfast and lunch but tea and supper were the responsibility of the prefects. The head girl arranged our table places and there was always great excitement to see who we were to sit next to. We all moved round one place each day, like the Madhatter's tea-party, but perhaps with more purpose. We all had a turn in sitting next to the staff and prefects and having our manners corrected and our conversation improved. As there was just one piece of cake each at teatime, we started with that to make sure of it. Bread and butter or bread and jam followed, but never both together. We were not allowed to help ourselves or ask for anything, we had to wait until our neighbour noticed that we had an empty plate. If our neighbour was very talkative we were apt to go hungry until a gentle nudge did the trick or we asked her very pointedly if she would like some bread when she had a large slice in front of her!

Although bread, butter and jam were never allowed together, one ingenious girl found a way round.

I had a setback over my plans for tea. We arrived back from an afternoon of games in the field, full of fresh air and ready for the large slices of bread and butter and bread and jam, but never butter *with* jam. So 1 had the bright idea of taking one of each and scraping the jam one's jam onto the butter one, but then there was the problem of disposing of the jamless bread. Others copied me at once, because it really was a good idea, but of course it was put down at once. No one gave me away as instigator, there was always a firm Fair Play attitude, and no one would sneak.

It is agreeable to see that the severe Miss Wilson of Chapter 1 knew what was what in the way of food.

By today's standards, the food was excellent and it far excelled food in other schools of the time. Miss Wilson was in some ways very enlightened. In summer there were large ample salads from the garden always arranged with eye-appeal, radishes being cut into the shape of water lilies. There was always the best olive oil too, with a superb flavour. In winter terms there would be plates of raw carrots at every High Tea, and all were expected to take one. Then for tea we might have scrambled egg on fried bread or pink porridge, which was minced ham on toast, or a delicious creamed haddock. Boiled eggs were served from a large basin and instead of egg cups we used our table napkin rings. There were plates of brown and white bread and butter and home made jam. On Tuesdays there were always Scotch pancakes (drop scones) and golden syrup. At weekends there were rock cakes, or chocolate sandwich and a mouth-watering moist gingerbread made with black treacle to a secret recipe of Miss Wilson. Everything was home made – nothing shop bought or canned. In the winter terms at Sunday High Tea there would always be huge bowls of hot vegetable soup full of succulent marrow-fat peas, to be eaten with bread and dripping from the joint. At lunch there were always ample roasts, stews and shepherd's pie, with accompanying vegetables, followed by the stodgy pudding which we all enjoyed in those days without consideration of waistlines, spots or levels of cholesterol. And there was always porridge for breakfast in the winter terms, and sausages on Sundays.

Our picnics were especially good. Groundsheets and rugs were spread out beneath the trees, hampers were unpacked and everyone was handed a lemonade bottle. Large home-made Cornish Pasties were passed round bursting with beef, potato, turnip and peas. These might be followed by crackly white rolls filled with tomato or banana, and sometimes the same spicy citron and sultana loaves we enjoyed in break, plus the famous school gingerbread.

Depressing though the following account of singularly sparse school food is, it is nevertheless pleasing to find that it resulted, however indirectly, in a surprising embonpoint among Old Girls.

There was no eating between meals because there was simply nothing to eat. There was a regulation arrowroot biscuit at 10.20 a.m. with yucky milk and another regulation biscuit of a slightly more substantial kind with even yuckier milk at 8.30 p.m. The 8.30 p.m. yucky milk had been delivered in the morning and had sat around all day so that by the time it was ready for consumption on a hot evening it resembled cheese rather than milk. Not for us the luxuries of refrigeration.

The penalties for disposing of this disgusting liquid in an unlawful fashion were extremely severe. The milk had to be drunk like a penance. It was as though at the end of the day we could purge ourselves of all sins that day and one glass of milk would make us physically and spiritually cleansed.

It was practically impossible to get to the cloakroom and tip it away, though not so difficult to pour it out of the window onto one poor withering, milk-sodden shrub which had found itself a target of some lucky disposers. The only way was to hold your nose and slug it down as fast as you could. Often this process was supervised just in case there was one milk left on the tray. If this ever happened there would be all hell let loose, and we would be stood in lines, in silence, indefinitely until the culprit owned up.

Because we were often so hungry, it is surprising that we did not relish this sour creamy liquid. Instead we ate acorns, chestnuts and what we called vinegar leaves. It was not until I had children of my own, collecting wild flowers for a project, that I discovered that our staple extra-curricula diet of vinegar leaves was in fact sorrel, described as an acid-leaved herb allied with the dock. How desperate we must have been!

The food was generally pretty sparse and disgusting with sugarless tea slopped from great urns to wash it down. The steamed roly-poly pudding which languished on an elongated tin tray was about twenty inches long. It earned the name of Dead Man's Leg when it was plain and Bugs in a Bolster when it was bestowed with currants.

Whatever was put before us we HAD to eat. One girl could not face boiled eggs, but she would sit there in solitary state with the cold boiled egg from breakfast time until lunchtime, or until she managed to push it down. She was made an example to us all, and woe betide anyone who might have thought about being fussy with their food. Unfortunately this has meant that we are now able, if not internally compelled, to finish up everything on *our* plates, on everyone else's plates or on any plate at every meal. This fact can be proved by the very large proportion of very large hips and very large bottoms which gather together on Old Girls Day.

Many will recall with delight the feverish excitement of dorm feasts. They were sometimes called 'midnight feasts' but usually took place about 10.25 p.m., the participants not having been able to bear to wait any longer.

—What I did enjoy were the midnight feasts especially those given by the rich farmers' daughters – rich cakes and oodles of Devonshire cream, sardines, sausage rolls etc. Unfortunately these came to an end one awful night when our rather special dorm (including two of the Headmistress's favourite sixth formers) was invaded by the Head herself. She had been informed of our venture by a very sly Maths mistress who must have overheard our plans. We had just got to the 'sweet' stage and were opening a large tin of peaches when the door opened and she marched in. Muriel, who was dishing out the fruit, lost her head and the juice poured out upon the floor, carrying Miss Beaumont with it. Oh dear! She had to be helped up and escorted to her room and was understandably furious. Apparently the sixth formers were blamed for showing such an example to us of the Lower Fourth and were quite inconsolable!

—We used to collect rather large crabs from the shore and take them back to the back door of the school kitchens, where a simple Irish lay sister would deposit them in a bath outside and promise to make them into fish cakes. Almost always the next day the crabs would have disappeared and we'd have fish in some form or other, always believing it was our mashed-up crabs. It was years later I discovered that they were taken back to the beach after we juniors were in bed and before the Grand Silence at 8.45 p.m.

Our plans and preparations for midnight feasts were interminable. The few day girls who came to the school were entrusted with the task of buying sickly cakes. On one occasion, when a trayload had been brought up to the school and hidden under a bed, we were about to start supper when Mother Superior appeared, called out our names and we were taken out into another room – St Binos – and there was our feast laid out and we had to eat it ALL there and then. All rooms were called after Saints or Titles of Our Lady. I slept in Our Lady of Mount Carmel.

I recall two puddings. One most school children

know – Flies Cemetery – was delicious, and so was Railway Smash, the most descriptive of titles – a large tin tray of flat, flat sponge, streaked in thin lines with red red jam!

I adored the dehydrated bananas we had for supper on many an occasion, but in my part of the refectory I was the only one who did and so everyone 'passed' theirs to me and what I couldn't eat I'd take out in my knickers for consumption later!

St Patrick's Day produced most interestingly coloured foods – green jelly, yellow custard, shamrock-shaped rolls with green jam and yellow butter etc.

—As I grew older I was promoted to living in the Annexe. We certainly got up to tricks; midnight feasts consisting of a revolting menu – sardines, oranges, sweets and playing 'snap' on the rugs. The loser was spun round and often landed under a bed – all the goodies were hidden up the chimney! I remember once I was the loser – I was spun round, the door opened and Miss Baggs (yes, that was her name) came in and I landed against her shins! My cowardly mates rushed to their respective beds and there was I alone to face the terror of Miss Baggs with her hair flowing down her back. Poor dear – she did not have time to scold – how could she – all I could say was, 'But your hair! Where's your bun?'

6

Games

Feelings about compulsory games vary greatly. Roughly speaking, those who were good at them liked them, and the duffers resented them as being a waste of time and effort. The perils and disadvantages of our national game came in for a lot of criticism.

There was a terrible fuss made about cricket as the games mistress, Miss Best, had 'played for England' or so the rumour went. She certainly *looked* as though she might have done, as her forearms had a lot of down on them and her legs were a bit hairy, not that that necessarily means that she was any good at cricket. Although she was a bit like a man, I never heard of anybody having a crush on her and during cricket she never stopped talking – 'Run up', 'Get that left leg forward', 'Back up', 'Well hit', 'Butterfingers!' etc, etc. We played with a proper cricket ball and took some nasty knocks. My B.F. (Best Friend) was then a very pretty girl called Cicely and she hated cricket and was an awful funk and was always afraid that the ball was going to knock her teeth out or break her nose or something. So one day, greatly daring, she asked Miss Best if we couldn't play cricket with a tennis ball as in Rounders. Miss Best nearly fainted, let out a shriek of horror and Cicely was sent to the Headmistress and was made to apologise to Miss Best, miss supper and

Miss Best had played for England or so the rumour went. She certainly looked as though she might have done . . .

write out 'I must try not to be so feeble' fifty times.

The following *cri de coeur* is characteristic of our anti-games correspondents, who were many in number and loud in protest.

> The school drill was supervised by gym mistresses, as they were known, and was a useful tool for them to display their sadistic natures. Hateful Hockey, Lousy Lacrosse, Nasty Netball, Tormenting Tennis and Revolting Rounders were not enough for them to inflict their tortures on the fat and flabby amongst us, the drill and gymnastics lessons gave them even more opportunities to reduce the non-athletic girls to total humiliation.
>
> It was good fortune to fall over and cut one's knee. Better still to fall on gravel as this would justify a large bandage for several days and exempted one from the undignified gymnastical acts. In horse-vaulting for instance, one would be expected to bounce on the spring-board and leap over the horse with a slight slap of the palms on the leather and fly through the air with zest and zeal, ending up with arms outstretched on a perfectly straight upright body. Unfortunately this did not work for some of us, who would find ourselves with fat, limp legs, obdurately hanging over the sides of the horse and our bottoms firmly plopped in the centre of its back. This was bad, but the mortifying part was then having to wriggle forwards doing the splits and try and get off this hateful equine structure.
>
> Rope climbing, wall bars, bar walking, high jump and other inflictions of severe bodily pain were thoroughly enjoyed by gym mistresses, who wielded enormous power. It is hard to imagine that they were probably little older than ourselves at the time.

At most schools it was customary to lavish praise and heap rewards on the best games players.

If you were good at sports you were a heroine. House and school colours (ribbons) were won and were sewn on the gym tunic. In our house, hockey and netball teams were addressed by the captain and tactics were discussed before a match. We foregathered in the play-room and the meeting was called a 'Foam', I have no idea why. Only if you were in the team were you allowed to know the secret ritual which ended a Foam. We would gather in a circle like a rugger scrum and kicking round a 'humpty' would chant:

Come on you Hillstow fighters
We'll beat the other blighters
We'll fight and scratch and win the match
Hurrah! Hurrah! Hurrah!

The reward for a match won was a Milky Way at supper time.

Sometimes, as one Headmistress reports, a keen games-playing parent lost his head.

Parents often had strange reasons for letting their daughters leave school. I think the strangest was when a father threatened to come and fetch his daughter if she were not immediately included in one of the tennis teams. This was not possible, so I had to point out that he had no more legal right to remove her without notice and without just cause than I had suddenly to send her away.

Games often alternated with what was then called Physical Drill, which led on to Figure Marching for which, from the spectator's point of view, a lofty perch was necessary for maximum enjoyment.

We never danced – we only marched. We had an ancient custom called school drill and this was per-formed on every high day and holiday to an overawed audience. Once a girl reached the age of about fourteen, she had to drill every Tuesday at noon for the rest of her school life. We dressed in white blouses and navy tunics which were so short they exposed not only our knees but our bulging muscular thighs too, of which we were very self-conscious. This was before the days of mini-skirts, of course, and the only girls in very short skirts then were either prostitutes or jolly good sporty types like us.

We marched into the hall, stood in straight lines and proceeded to do a series of exercises to music supplied by two piano teachers thumping on the old Bechstein in the corner. The worst exercise was the knee-bending one, when a cacophony of kneejoints cracking would fill the hall. Unfortunately not all the knees cracked in unison and the cracking would sound like a round of shots being let off from a barrage of pistols. After these exercises, designed to give us good postures, big busts, firm thighs and pancake-flat stomachs, were completed we had to march into formations and patterns. This wondrous effort when viewed from the balcony would bring forth warm applause.

Swimming was popular, though there could be problems in the days before heated pools and the generally de luxe bathing conditions that seem to be both expected and provided nowadays.

As today's schoolgirls enjoy the delights of a heated swimming pool, they can have little idea of what it was like to have swimming lessons in the sea off Cranmer, but those who suffered from them will never forget. The current at Cobbold's Point, sweeping inexorably past, swirls dangerously round the cliff at high tide, with a vicious backlash. Remains of an old seaplane pier and stone breakwaters are strewn along the shore but the obvious dangers did not deter the College prospectus from advertising sea-bathing as an added attraction. Staff gallantly took on the weighty responsibility of swimming lessons in the sea. An old summerhouse on the cliff housed the changing rooms, one for wet and the other for dry girls. Half a class swam at a time and wet and dry got hopelessly muddled, so that Old Girls can remember soggy wet dresses, and a mess of mud and sand on the floors, after many feet, in bathing shoes, had tramped back up the path to the summerhouse, bringing a trail of seawater with them.

The undertow was so dangerous that the girls swam in a rectangle with two rowing-boats marking its boundary. At best, it was a cold dash in, a splash about for ten minutes and then came the whistle for 'out'. Girls often came out of the water with grazed shins and knees and cut toes! Swimming instruction was given by a mistress while balancing in one of the boats and shouting through a megaphone, always on the alert lest she needed to dive in and life-save.

Elsewhere softies got short shrift!

—Sport was not neglected in the school at this time. Swimming was arranged at the local public baths, but the girls could attend only on special days and the water had to be changed beforehand. Girls who could not, or would not, go in were thrown in!

—In the summer we never bathed in the sea, but in Brill's Baths. I cannot imagine why this dreadful proceeding had to take place at break of day, but we always started in cabs at 6.30 a.m. The baths filled me with horror, but I suppose I was made to go. Our bathing dresses extended from neck to knee with a belt and sleeves and were usually made of thick serge. I never bathed from Brighton beach though we went down to the sea quite often in the holidays. It was fun to watch people mount into the queer old bathing machines and then a horse would

pull the lumbering contrivance right into the water
and the bather emerged from the sea end opposite
the door which formed the entrance. There were
dreadful old women in voluminous blue serge skirts,
who ducked frightened children and made whole
families stand in rows holding hands. Very often
only their feet were in the water.

When neither sea nor swimming baths were available, home-
made alternatives were resorted to:

The reason was boredom once more, but this time it
was in mid-summer. My parents and I were still resident in Southport and one of my most enjoyable activities in those days was the seaside paddling. So, being
with my boarding companions on a rather sweltering
evening, I thought: 'Wouldn't it be lovely if we could
do some paddling here in the dormitory!' We had a
floor covered with a firm layer of linoleum, on which
some rugs were positioned down the centre and between the beds. Against the outer wall there were four
wash-basins for our night and morning ablutions.

Yes! You've guessed it! With no hesitation and obviously little forethought we all got to work removing
the rugs and turning on the taps. With the four basins
plugged, in no time at all our dormitory was trans-
formed into a seaside resort, and we were cooling and
regaling ourselves by cavorting in the few inches of
water.

When sleeping time arrived, we used one or two
available plastic buckets to remove some of the pool
contents and the remaining moisture, as I had planned
in advance, was meticulously mopped up by some
bagsful of sheets and pillowcases waiting to be collected
for despatch to the laundry. (We had changed our bed
linen that very day. Everything well timed!) So we
replaced the rugs, retired to our beds and slept peace-

fully in premises which had been returned to their former shipshape condition.

Morning came, we awoke and dressed as usual. BUT, we had only been at the breakfast table in the dining hall a few minutes when a very disturbed elderly teacher rushed in to inform the Headmistress, seated at the top of one of the four, long tables, that there had been a leakage from the ceiling above the extension classroom. A further 'strange happening' was announced later in the morning by another teacher. She had been dealing with the laundry items and had found them 'sopping wet'!

At this point, of course, I just had to make a remorseful confession. In my naïveté I had never at the time realised that there was, inevitably, a narrow space between floor and skirting-board through which much of our flood would seep into the classroom below. My intentions had been to please my colleagues and myself entirely harmlessly. I would never have contemplated such a thing had I known the potential outcome.

It is odd to find that lacrosse, surely rather a dangerous game when compared with, say, netball, was so highly rated by one mother and for an unusual reason.

My mother, whose sole aim where I was concerned was that I should grow in all the arts and crafts which would eventually ensnare a rich husband or, rather, enable her to ensnare one for me, had – in order to safeguard my beauty (not in any case my most promising art or craft) – forbidden me to play hockey because it was rough and dangerous; but I might play lacrosse because it would make me graceful. Where she got these curious ideas it is hard to imagine, but on the whole it was a good thing she was never on the sidelines on a dripping icy darkling December afternoon, to see the churning mud, the charging lumping bodies and the pouring sweat of muddied oafs who owed nothing at all to Kipling.

Distant playing fields provided hazards.

'Games' was a horror I did my best to avoid. The school used a hockey pitch about a mile away, easily located by following the hordes of 'flashers' lining our route. Tennis was taught on the local club's courts and mainly involved cries of 'Sorry'. One American girl was a really excellent player, but this was considered not quite 'on' since her play involved staff and girls running around quite unnecessarily. I think there was also netball. There was most definitely swimming before breakfast in the summer in the local open air pool and not even youth, nor the regulation royal blue costume, provided immunity to cold.

Once again a father interfered, but this time to some purpose.

Ravensmead was a 'lacrosse' school, the main reason I was sent there, since in his youth Father had played the game for the South of England and he was determined I should follow in his footsteps.

It was greatly to my advantage that I am left-handed, thus confusing the opposition who expected my 'lax' stick to be waving above my right shoulder; added to this, Father's past experience proved invaluable – first he chose a 'Lally', a vastly superior breed of lacrosse stick, then he cut a good fifteen inches off the handle, making it a truly fearsome, one-handed weapon. He then spent a considerable amount of time and effort soaking the basket in oil and thumping at it with his heel, till it looked more than anything like an old lady's shopping bag. Then he told me to go forth and play Third Man, the plum defence position. It was a winner! Never fleet of foot I thundered up and down the turf, the ball so firmly wedged in the shopping basket that even I had trouble in getting rid of it when there was a call to 'PASS!'

In quite a short space of time I was promoted to the first team, promoted to Early Lunch on Saturdays (reserved for the elite going off to play in matches), to the joy of team spirit as we sang 'Frère Jacques' from the comfort of the hired motor coach, and Team Tea on our return, reliving the match, basking in our own glory whenever we won – which we usually did.

Only one school regularly defeated us – St Winifred's. Time after time we set off to do battle, amazons who for weeks had fallen out of bed at first light, run out into the biting winter morning, 'lax' sticks akimbo, to practise picking-up and passing, shooting, intercepting and cradling, all to no avail. 'St Winny's', beaten at tennis and netball, even occasionally at swimming, remained triumphant on the 'lax' field.

Father minded about this perennial defeat almost as much as we did, and it was he who finally hit upon the means of salvaging our honour. 'Tell the girls there's a prize,' he said. 'If they win on Saturday I will personally present them with a five-pound box of Fuller's chocolates.'

Bribery of that sort, to a team starved of the most primitive luxuries, proved sufficient – the white box with the wide red ribbon dangling metaphorically before our eyes, we launched into battle, pulverising the opposition, storming the length of the field, Left Defence Wing to Centre to Right Attack to Second Home, First Home and – 'GOAL!' Three times we did it till hot and sweaty and gasping for breath we gathered around the 'Winny's' girls, sportingly shook hands, assured them 'It was only luck!' – then to a man, turned and fled to the car where Father sat, the door open, the Fuller's chocs on his knee.

For a girl who heartily disliked all games, the following episode is particularly disagreeable.

A few days before my eleventh birthday, we were halfway through breakfast when Miss Wilson shouted out to me, who was then sitting at Miss Harcourt's table (we all moved on one place every day), 'Jane Holmes, your grandmother has written to me to ask what you would like for your birthday. I have told her you would like a cricket bat; and I have therefore bought you an Autograph.' My heart sank with disgust. Autograph was a very choice bat, but it was not one of my aspirations, and I loathed cricket, mainly out of loyalty to my father who always spoke disparagingly of the 'flannelled fools'. He, having been a delicate child, had had a tutor at home and at university he had rowed and played rugger, so cricket had not come his way.

Miss Wilson continued to add to my mortification by announcing in front of the school that Granny's cook had baked me a birthday cake, but that she could not possibly allow me to have it as it was too small for the school to share and she also suspected it would be too rich. She would therefore return it. How I envied other girls who on their birthdays had enormous orange or chocolate iced cakes delivered from Dumpers. Miss Wilson would cut the cake into thirty huge slices and they would be eaten in almost sacramental silence and with much enjoyment.

When my birthday arrived I was presented by Miss Wilson with the despised bat and, later, sitting at the trestle tables for High Tea, Granny's cake was suddenly produced, pronounced not too rich after all and cut into thirty shamingly small slices, so that I felt humiliated and embarrassed.

In avoiding games, some were more cunning than others.

Our school suffered from underground cloakrooms, where we kept our wellingtons, macs, racquets, and dreaded hockey boots. I detested hockey, and those dreary descents to the 'Abode of the Damned', in the winter terms, were agony! My only escape was to spend so long down there, looking for a 'lost' hockey boot that, mercifully, the coach full of players used to leave without me – then I had to creep back up into civilisation, without being too obviously spotted. But, clearly, one couldn't do this too often.

I regret to report in one school a particularly bad games 'tone'.

The day proceeded normally with lessons, and there was a brief pause for the Angelus at 12 p.m. After lunch/dinner, in silence, we would look to see if we were 'down for games'. I have to admit I detested organised games and joined a subversive group on the field. We would ostensibly participate in the game of lacrosse (thought to be more graceful than hockey), and put on our colours. We would then ignore the ball and discuss Auden, MacNeice, Isherwood, the War poets, the Sitwells . . . If one's name was missing, a walk in crocodile formation was arranged. Girls must walk in threes and two girls escorted the nun in charge, one on either side. Now we could question the nun and, although she would seldom tell us of her life before entering the convent, she would describe Nigeria if she had been on the foreign missions. We came to know odd little bits about West Africa whilst plodding along the Leeds road.

It is a relief to find that modesty was sometimes prized well above proficiency at games.

We played hockey, netball and tennis – but genteelly – modesty being of the essence. In fact, on windy days, we were required to wear the girdles of our gymslips somewhere near the bottom, close to our knees, to prevent them blowing up and depriving onlookers of a glimpse of our undergarments. Sport, on windy days, wasn't played too well in this hobbled state!

One so fears that, in the case of the following girl, the rest of her life represented a sad anti-climax.

The games captain was adored by all – or nearly all – and strode around with her admirers carrying her hockey stick, tennis racquet etc behind.

Back again to yet another anti-gamesite.

To me the ultimate hell was hockey in mid-winter on a muddy field with a keen wind blowing straight through my jersey, flannel blouse, liberty bodice and woollen combinations. The despairing games mistress, alias the Lady Matron, tried me in various positions on the field and finally put me in goal, where I whiled away the time by morbidly digging little holes with my hockey stick. How I welcomed those times in the month when I was 'off games'. This was the school's sole concession to feminine frailty, and very welcome it was too.

It is indeed pleasant to end on an enthusiastic note.

The summer terms were lovely and dominated by cricket matches which I adored and I kept my own private scores. There were other visiting teams, but the great event of the season was the Fathers' Match. One year we were proud to feature in a cartoon in *Punch* (Oh, why did I not keep a copy?!!). There was the school in the distance – all of us in our djibbahs and a member of the school team clinging on to her father's arm and whispering – 'Daddy, when you get out, make it LBW, it looks so much better than caught or run out.'

7

Worship

It pains me to have to report that the memories of Sundays, church services, collect-learning, Bible-reading, prayers and religion in general are almost uniformly depressed and depressing. Shudders are everywhere. Dismay is freely expressed at the waste of time, the often unctuous and unreal discourses, the purposely induced guilt feelings that caused such misery and, above all, the boredom. Many a horse (or in this case I suppose we should say mare) had been led to the water but few had drunk, or drunk with profit. 'As you sow, you are like to reap' sounds vaguely Biblical but is in fact Samuel Butler (the *b.* 1612 one) and is here a woefully inaccurate statement for who down the years can have sown more faithfully and diligently for this derisory harvest than schoolmistresses without number, backed up by vicars, chaplains, rectors, lay preachers and every manner of divine. Here there is cause for grief (do Bishops grieve? They seldom *look* as though they spent much time at it. Perhaps it's the fancy dress and the permanently carnival appearance) and, being grievous, the instances of dissatisfaction have here been limited.

How old-fashioned nowadays are orderly 'crocodiles' of prim schoolgirls parading to or from church? One can but think that they still exist, for how else to shepherd in an orderly manner a giggling, chattering mob of seventy or more, dressed in their Sunday best and destined for worship? Time was when such processions were customary and caused no comment.

—The walks along the Promenade after Church on Sundays were feats of organisation and planning by Mrs Lane. All the girls had to wear their Sunday outfits of cream suits, with everything to match. They then proceeded to the College Gardens where they were paired off exactly to height and to the length of their skirts. The crocodile would then set off, with the tallest girls leading the way. There was to be a gap of exactly one yard between each pair, and Mrs Lane inspected the crocodile as it passed to ensure that this requirement was observed – a light tap with a cane serving to bring the wayward back into position. This became one of the shows of the town.

—We had to file out two by two to Church on Sundays like animals going out of the ark. Matins was compulsory, Holy Communion optional – no guesses for which we preferred! There was a school lore known only to ourselves – implicitly believed but in retrospect totally ridiculous. If one ate brown bread one would produce twins and if one stuffed one's shoes with wet blotting paper one would faint in prayers. My kid-lined evening shoes bore ink stains for years!

—Sunday was an occasion for serious thought and reflection. The whole school attended a private morning service at the local Wesleyan chapel; this was held at 10 a.m., I think, before the public worship at eleven. After service the school formed into four or five crocodiles and proceeded for the Sunday Walk along the promenade, dressed in Sunday Outfits: navy coats and white hats in winter, white coats, hats and gloves in summer. It was one of the sights of the seaside town to see The Young Ladies of the college taking their walk.

On returning to school we had an hour of 'Hymn Learning'; a hymn was allotted for the day, each girl took a hymn book, the hymn was learnt and repeated to the supervising mistress.

Sunday lunch was cold and was followed by an afternoon rest before what was known as 'Class' which was a form of Sunday School when we had the lives of saints and missionaries expounded to us. The evening was given over to letter writing (supervised, of course) followed by more hymn singing and early bed.

—There was no Chapel until 1935 so, on Sundays, the School walked in crocodile, escorted by Staff, to the parish church of St Peter and St Paul. Although it must have been something of an event simply to get out of the school grounds, the chief memories which girls have of 'Church parade' are dreary ones. We all hated the weekly visit to the old parish church even when it was enlivened by Miss Gilbert saying: 'Cross straight over to the White Horse when you come out of church.'

Nor was the walk, still in crocodile, along the Promenade, any more popular, though this filled in the gap between Matins and lunch. Walks along the Prom I hated but they could be cheered up if three or four girls combined to get chocolate out of a machine without being seen by the member of Staff at the end of the croc. It not only involved co-operation but the extreme wickedness of keeping back a penny from Church collection, as we never handled any money. Our shopping was done for us and we were not allowed any sweets.

—We welcomed Sunday morning Church parade. We wore our own, varied Sunday bests, and real hats, and carried prayer books, and one penny of our precious sixpence pocket money and went to the parish church. There, from our group of pews, we could see some of the boys from the school, in their segregated group. We enjoyed the various visiting ministers – a Mr Fawkes who whistled through his teeth, and a darling old man, who dwelt ponderously on names, such as Shadrach, Meshach and Abednego. We raced spiders along the pews, and got warning taps on our shoulders. The worst disaster was for one of us to faint – utter disgrace, which brought a heavier than usual dose from Matron that evening. Sunday evening service was held in school with our Head enjoying herself to the full, sermonising. Another penny from our precious sixpence had to be given to a collection.

As some girls have sad cause to know, walking abroad occasionally had peculiar perils of its own.

I remember leading the school 'croc' to Church one Sunday in summer. There we were, in our Rosy Pearls, a double line of about fifty virgins and there, at a street corner, by a lamp post, was a man in a waving, loose macintosh!

For all my ignorance, I knew instinctively that here was a threat! I was head girl, I was leading the crocodile. What to do? Stop? Turn round and put the croc in reverse and be late at St John's? I did what any true English woman would have done – I gritted my teeth, averted my eyes and soldiered on!

The waving macintosh waved no more. There were no screams, no scuffles behind me, so presumably the sight of so much innocence had deflated his ego. Our ignorance remained unsullied!

The old-fashioned Sunday certainly had its perils and tribulations.

My first Summer Term was lived on a knife edge, every minute held a potential time bomb. What with being constantly sent back to the lavatory, late baths, stripped beds and having to re-copy smudged homework before I could get it signed, I seldom finished

There we were, a double line of fifty virgins, and there was a man in a waving, loose macintosh!

prep by the allotted time. Learning homework had to be heard and passed as correct. This was not usually a problem as I learnt easily. It was Miss Wilson who heard our Old Testament learning. No errors were allowed, you had to be word perfect and awe of Miss Wilson could lead to temporary amnesia. She could prove difficult to get hold of, and if the work was not heard before Prayers you had to try and catch her after breakfast, and this she did not like.

Once I was reciting to Miss Wilson 'Will the Lord be pleased with thousands of rams with ten thousand rivers of oil? Shall I give my firstborn for my transgression, the fruit of my body for the sin of my soul? He hath shown thee, O man, what is right.' Here Miss Wilson put down the Bible and peered over her spectacles at a Senior girl who had just come in. 'Veronica,' she bellowed, 'I have a bone to pick with you. I hear you kicked the cat downstairs this morning.' 'Yes, Miss Wilson.' 'Come and see me after prep.' She picked up the Bible. 'Go on, Jane Holmes.' But, intrigued by the tale of the cat, I had lost the thread and it was not until the middle of the night that 'What doth the Lord require of thee but to do justly, love mercy and walk humbly with thy God' surfaced to my brain.

After Sunday breakfast we changed into tussore dresses, white socks and pork-pie hats with black bands (in winter we were a colourful motley of velveteen). Three-quarters of the school would be going to Holy Trinity with Miss Wilson, the lucky remainder to St Thomas's with Miss Harris. Holy Trinity was known as 'very High' and was, according to Miss Wilson, vastly superior to any other Service, being the Service given by Jesus. Matins at 'Low Church St Thomas's' was decidedly inferior.

Quite arbitrarily, I was assigned to Holy Trinity. I had never been to a Communion Service before,

coming from an Anglo-Irish Protestant family whose
children did not go to the Service before Confirmation.
The Service started at 10 a.m. and before we formed
into croc we were each handed a small paper book of
faded orange entitled 'Our Bounden Duty'.

Holy Trinity was in those days in a rather impover-
ished part of the town but the Church was well attended and as we walked past the Rood Cross and up
to the north door Miss Wilson would stride ahead into
the porch while we all came to a halt, drew out clean
handkerchiefs and on the command 'Blow', blew our
noses. From then on till the end of the Service, coughing
and nose blowing were forbidden.

After Sunday lunch we had an hour's rest out of
doors on our rugs, reading. And after High Tea there
would be hymn singing in the drawing-room with Miss
Wilson playing the piano. This led on to Prayers and
bedtime.

A pleasingly quaint experience awaited one ailing confirmand.

After Pearl Harbor, there was an American Air Force
station only a mile or two distant and the girls were
often wakened in the early hours by the revving up of
the Flying Fortresses based there. One afternoon, as
they were playing hockey, the teams were horrified to
see a Fortress crash in flames and the sight haunted
them for many nights to come. On a lighter note, I
had mumps while I was being prepared for Confirmation. It was thought that I had better attend the last
class but, as I was officially still in quarantine, I had
to sit on a stepladder, outside the window of the room
where the class was being held. On that particular
afternoon, the Forts were extremely noisy and I heard
not one word that the Vicar was saying.

Some religious denominations were considerably more demanding than others, and sometimes alarmingly so.

We were expected to go to sleep at night (in case we were 'Called' during the night) in a 'holy' attitude. This necessitated folding one's arms across one's breast. The word bust was not in our vocabulary. Most girls didn't have one anyway, and those who did were considered to be somewhat freakish and to be pitied, because they couldn't possibly be considered 'sporty' by the rest of us, the criterion by which we lived.

Our clothes had to be arranged in the form of a crucifix over the backs of our chairs, which were then placed neatly and tidily by our beds. We dressed and undressed beneath our dressing gowns draped over our shoulders like cloaks. We faced inwards, towards the beds, for fear of catching sight of naked flesh. It was all very, very difficult, particularly when doing up one's liberty bodice and suspenders.

The nuns did indeed bathe through a hole in a tent-like contraption placed as a frame over their bath.

We were woken in the mornings by a nun visiting each bed with an old paste-pot, in which was a sponge soaked in Holy Water. As she approached each bed, she thrust the Holy Water at you and said 'Benedicamus Domino' – and we had to reply 'Deo Gratias', and take Holy Water and make the sign of the Cross. Woe betide anyone who didn't respond immediately. Some nuns would actually squeeze the Holy Water over your face.

We were constantly praying for Holy Deaths.

And, of course, we bought Black Babies, a practice I have since wondered about. A black baby in Africa cost 2/6d, so we saved to do it. In all I must have about twenty 35-year-old women in Africa. The 2/6d enabled a black baby to be Christened, and for you to name the black baby – all mine were called Imelda Therese. If anyone travels in Africa and comes across an Imelda Therese, she's mine!

One particular nun, who told us that St Joseph was
the patron Saint of fine weather, would push his statue
out into the quad when a fine day was needed – put
up an umbrella over him, and we would walk round
in a circle chanting a litany. Strangely it never did
rain. We spent a good deal of time in Chapel and
were forever celebrating feast days and Holy Days of
Obligation, which some of us called Hobbly Gobbly
days.

In the midst of so much obedience and conformity it is splendid
to find an occasional rebel.

We had a tremendously daring girl called Beryl who
ran every kind of risk. She didn't care a hoot about
anything and we all envied her. After tea (the last
meal) on Sundays there was an hour when we were
supposed to improve our minds. As far as I can recall,
the rather fancy name for it was 'Devotional Reading'
or something and we were meant to read lives of the
Saints or a biography of Florence Nightingale or 'On
a Bicycle Through the Holy Land' – things like that
(the school library was full of them). Beryl had got
from somewhere one of those leather book jacket things
that you used to wrap round books (this was sixty
years ago) to keep them clean, especially library books,
and inside it she would put the latest Ethel M. Dell or
whatever she could get hold of that was exciting and
readable. And to put the mistresses off the scent (we
were all 'on our honour' so they didn't snoop around
very much) she painted a white title on the leather
jacket and it said QUIET THOUGHTS FOR QUIET TIMES.
Beryl was very enterprising in all sorts of ways and
gingered things up whenever she could. The Headmistress doted on her, little realising what a rogue she
really was, and it was no surprise to anybody when at

the end of the summer term Beryl was awarded the cup for The Girl Who Has Done Most – quite a customary title in those days, but really rather odd when you come to think about it.

To rebel in another and more sensitive matter required courage of a high order.

Brought up in a 'low Church' family, it was a shock to my parents to be told in my first letter: 'We went to church this morning and the incense made me cough.' The Headmistress, fanatically religious, and an ardent Anglo-Catholic, did not take kindly to my forming a splinter group to attend a less 'high' service in another church. Soon, half the school joined me in going to St John's instead of enduring the smells and bells at St Peter's, and I was never forgiven for having been the cause of this schism.

Elsewhere, incense was much more popular.

Normal life revolved around Church, saints and feast days. I learnt the whole of the catechism at the age of five and to my sister's surprise got the catechism prize.
Reverend Mother's feast was when the nuns wore clean bonnets and we wore our white silk dresses, had hot rolls and honey for breakfast, no lessons but High Mass and a procession. We loved processions, especially when it was fine, as we walked down the aisle, out of the end door and round the gardens singing hymns and throwing rose petals, with Father Humboldt shaking incense. He had been abroad for nine years. He lived with Madame Cécile, his housekeeper, who was very fat and smelt. He was very generous and used to call me into the sacristy on my way out of church and stuff toffees up my knickers.

A few random reminiscences will help to fill in the fairly strange picture.

— Every Thursday a curate came to take a service. Miss Plum played the harmonium. She was very stout and overflowed through the back of her bench. Each evening she took Prayers, standing at a portable lectern. We had to leave the room backwards, and curtsey at the door.

— I remember one Good Friday we went to the Parish Church for a 10.30 service and then to the three-hour service from 12 – 3. It was too far to return home in the interval, so we waited in the churchyard and ate hot-X buns which we had brought and kept hidden in our hats or the fronts of our blouses.

— When we were not in Church listening to Fr. Antonine, or praying, we read holy books. I picked the lives of the saints, especially the martyrs, as they had some gory bits in and were less boring than theology.

— We prayed and prayed like parrots. Collecting pleniary indulgences, six Our Fathers, six Hail Marys and six Glory Bes for the Pope's intentions. Spiritual Bouquets for Rev. Mother's feast day – each prayer was a flower and we marked them up before the day and gave them to her together with an earthly bouquet and a speech!

— Television was almost unheard of. We were allowed to see a religious programme on Sundays and, if the Pope or a Bishop came on, we all had to kneel in front of the TV! Sundays were a nightmare, a sedate walk around the cemetery with white gloves and a dress with a lace collar – two-by-two – was the high spot. We prayed for rain on these walks. Sunday was Chapel. We wore white veils on Sundays (blue for the rest of the week), our right shoes cracked across the toes with so much genuflecting.

—Two or three times a year, Corpus Christi being one
of them, we all dressed in white and paraded through
the streets of this North Country town singing Ave
– Ave – Ave – Maria etc, etc, behind statues and
banners. We were the object of ridicule by the
local children (I don't blame them) but it was so
embarrassing. To make matters worse we all carried
assorted single flowers. On one of these humiliating
occasions I discovered that if you ate an iris flower
your tongue swelled up dramatically – maybe it was
only me!

—Once we had a Jesuit priest staying with us for a
week. An aura of holiness hung over the school.

Apart from taking services, this imposing six-foot
priest would sit at certain times in the Chapel,
available as a kind of spiritual Marjorie Proops.

I was head girl and did my best to beat up
custom. When it became apparent that no one had a
problem, I felt I couldn't let the side down. So armed
with a trumped-up domestic problem I went myself.
He listened, we prayed – and then he kissed me! I
came out scarlet faced, quite sure that when I said
'Grace' at tea, the whole school would guess what
had happened!

—On Sundays – in virgin white – we attended Church,
as did boys from another Public School near by. A
pretty girl, Joan, was apprehended passing notes to
one of the latter, a handsome youth. Her parents
were sent for and she was *removed*. I became friendly
with her remaining two sisters – Londoners like
myself – jolly and more interested in school life than
Joan. However, what was my surprise when one day
I was asked to come to the English mistress's study
– a charming woman – and told to keep away from
them or I wouldn't get the Form's English prize!

Her parting words seemed very inept: 'Following
pitch maketh one defiled'! I'm afraid I didn't take
her advice, but got the prize.

—There were several customs which were handed
down for many years. On Saturday night at Prayers
a certain number of girls read a text which they had
chosen on some given subject. One Saturday, the
subject must have been flowers, and a very plain
and spotty girl rose and declaimed in stentorian
tones 'I am the rose of Sharon and the lily of the
valley.'

But here and there the seed, so conscientiously sown, did fall
into good ground and we can end on a note of hope and of
success.

I was confirmed young, aged twelve, in Exeter Cathedral by Bishop Mortimer (I was in the same form as
Katharine Mortimer, the Bishop's Dortimer!). Wonderful – I am eternally grateful to my parents that I
went to schools in two cathedral cities. I used to
love the atmosphere, the services, and the eccentrics,
including one ancient Canon at Salisbury who
wouldn't have females sitting near him, so we had to
avoid his stall! The concerts in Salisbury Cathedral
were heavenly, despite the hard chairs, the draughts
and the general cold (unless you were next to one of
those enormous boilers). My only complaint was that
we didn't go often enough to the Cathedral – usually
we had to attend a very 'high' Church, the Rector of
which was supposed to be the school chaplain (he
came to the school sometimes to hear confessions, an
amenity of which I never took advantage). There was
a monthly School Service, which was only for the school
and was a very elaborate Sung Eucharist complete with
incense etc. – smells and bells or pongs and gongs. My
friend Alison and I became Servers in the sixth form

because it made the service slightly more interesting, except when you were dreaming and forgot to bang the gong. One terrible year Easter was very early and we had to stay at school over it. We had a two-hour ordeal on Good Friday (or was it on Easter Eve?) consisting of candles lit and unlit, and lots of incomprehensible chanting. I wonder how many people were put off church-going for life by all this – I wasn't, but I came from a clerical family!

8

Letters

Memory can sometimes be an unreliable agent but at least in the carefully preserved letters from school memory is not involved and it is the plain truth we are getting, occasionally of a kind that parents would find distressing.

Dearest Darlingest Mummy,

I hope you will come and see me when you come home if you don't I shall yell the place down, (A Threat). but honestly you must come. I got my uniform yesterday morning, I don't think the weather is what you would call beatiful.

I don't think I have ever slept in such an uncumfy bed before. Isn't it funny that I should sleep with Thelma Dodd. The two other girls names are Hazel Green and Betty O'Connell. I do wish I were coming home I am terribly lonely without you and Daddy. The food is disgustingly bad. The attention of going to the lavotry is very bad, there is always something going on when you want to to.

I am in IVB and am youngest at school.

Please give my best love to Auntie Hawken and Uncle and Joyce.

Don't you think its awful they don't provide you with soap so Hazel had to lend me some. I am not having as good a time as I thought I would.

Betty Gordan said I was to thank you for bringing her down in the car. Mummy you've simply got to come and see me, I'll think it jolly mean if you don't. Guides are tomorrow night. I felt terribly homesick this morning. I'm sure its a waste of money sending me here so I hope to come home and stay home after this term. The beastly food makes me sick if I eat any too. So please bring me home.

   With tons and tons of love to you and Daddy from your lonely

                    Pat

           xxxxxxxxxxxxxx

Please send me a FEW letters

One doubts whether the above letter was ever seen by Authority, the usual custom being that a mistress diligently perused all outgoing mail.

> You couldn't say anything nasty about the place as we weren't allowed to seal up our letters and they all had, at Sunday tea, to be handed in to Miss Ingle for her to read later on (and miss a post). Sometimes you got ticked off for bad handwriting. I imagine that a lot of our letters were pretty boring – hockey match scores and so on – but you never got ticked off for being boring, which would have been more sensible.

It was not only letters to parents that were subjected to censorship. A system was evolved for preventing unsatisfactory correspondence with others. Boys, of course.

> All letters not to our family had to be sent home first, unsealed, so that our parents could read what we had put, thus removing any chance of a first romance! I did get letters from a boy at Charterhouse, the school crest was always on the envelope, and the other girls giggled over this. It rather pleased me to pretend that they were love letters – actually they were entirely about cricket and couldn't have been more boring! But

the HM with her eagle eye noticed and she wrote to
my parents, who wrote back in some distress at my
behaviour. I must admit that I was never really afraid
of the HM and I burst into her study and accused her
of underhanded behaviour in writing to my parents,
without first giving me a chance to defend myself. I
think it quite took the wind out of her sails.

One writer reports a particularly dreary addition to the Sunday
letter.

Every Sunday between first and second mass we wrote
to our parents. These letters were left open for our
form mistress to put in our conduct cards. The conduct
cards were of different colours and there were bad
marks for 4 categories: Neatness, Application, Conduct
and Politeness. No marks – you got a blue card. I had
one blue card for the whole of my school career and at
weekly proclamation the whole school clapped. Under
11 marks in one or all categories you got a pink card,
12 or more a yellow card, something very bad gave
you a green card. No card was the biggest disgrace.

Fortunately there are ways of getting round rules and regulations.

Once a month we were allowed to write to friends, but
they were read so you couldn't write to boys. We
devised a plan to write to each other's brothers and
put the letters in our parents letters. I wrote to Donagh
Cush's brother Desmond who sounded a very dull boy.
My letter was also out of the ordinary. I am 12 years
old, brown hair, 4 foot whatever and I like hockey and
collect stamps and so on. Off went all the letters
undetected and we awaited results with secret glee.

Some of the other girls got letters, but it was my
second letter that caused all the trouble. Staying in
Desmond's parents house was a French boy of 18 and
I received a long letter written in French and adorned

at the top with 2 little hearts with an arrow through them. During 'second breakfast' we were trying to decypher the French when the nun in charge, Madame Maria, came up looking very angry and said 'Give me that letter.' 'I can't,' I said, but it was snatched out of my hand and borne off to Reverend Mother.

In a voice of doom she said out loud for all to hear, 'DOROTHY, YOUR MOTHER IS IN THE PARLOUR.'

My Mother and Father were indeed in the parlour. Reverend Mother had sent for them. I was well on the way to becoming a prostitute. 'Mrs Glencross, it was a real love letter, you know.' Luckily my Mother thought it a huge joke and a great fuss about nothing and after duly tut-tutting we all went out for tea.

The letters provide in general a splendid cross-section of experience, the full warp and woof of scholastic life. There are requests for food ('By the way, I have nearly finished my marmite and half my lemon curd'). There are pranks ('Katy and I have just made an apple-pie bed for someone') of one kind or another ('A girl in my dorm streaked in our room last night!'). There are worries about losing girlish figures ('Tomorrow there is Weighing. I'll probably find that I am very HEAVY!'). There is, but only very rarely, gratitude ('Thank you so much for sending me here, it really is super'). There are mishaps at lacrosse ('I have an enormous bruise on the side of my knee') and at other games ('Miss Mason got a rounders ball in her eye and it is all colours of the rainbow, mostly black'). There are social engagements ('Lulu has asked me to her birthday party, and so had Carol, as well as a girl called Laura Pelham, so I'm quite booked!!'). There is crime ('The latest scandal in the school so far is that last weekend some girls broke into the store cupboard in the kitchen. Some owned up.'). There is no racism ('I am in Form III2B and our form mistress seems to be a cross between a Siamese and Indian type, but she is quite nice'). There are intellectual

'Miss Mason got a rounders ball in her eye and it is all colours of the rainbow, mostly black.'

failures ('Because I was bottom in History, Miss Collins said "Well, Anne, 'Blessed is he who expecteth little'." I got 21%'). There are artistic misfortunes ('I went sketching. I did not shine. We did the crucifix in the cemetery and mine went all blotchy'). There are plenty of those friendships that wax and wane ('My favourite friend is called Susie. Anyway I don't know if I should have said that as we are hardly on speaking terms because of a row!!').

Naughtiness on the following scale is rather rare, or anyway goes unreported.

> Last Sunday it was our housemistress's weekend off and so some people in my house snooped about in her room and drank some of her wine and took one of her bottles of sherry. I don't know if she has found out about it yet.
>
> We all had to go to the parish church on Sunday, which was awful. Once a term the whole school has to go to Church, otherwise we have a really short service every sunday in the Chapel.
>
> Did you watch Diamonds are Forever last sunday night? In the beginning only the top two years were going to be allowed to watch it, but everyone was furious and so they let the whole school watch it.
>
> Anyway I must go to my Physics lesson now . . .

It is very reassuring to find girls alert for enemies in what can only be a wartime letter.

> We are *convinced* one of the staff is a spy. Did I tell you that last week? I hope not. Anyway she's most queer (Miss Miller, biology mistress) and puts coloured sticks and large water-jugs in her bedroom window, *we* think for signs. And she's always prowling around in a suspicious way and disappearing and altogether a shady character. We have a news bulletin on the board and whenever anybody thinks they've found out some valuable information they post it up there.

Was poor Miss Miller duly posted up? One imagines so. Who could resist this charming exuberance or fail to respond to the culinary request that accompanies it?

> Darling, Darling, Darling Mummy and Daddy.
>
> Well, all the French exams are finished now and weren't at all bad! – only 3 to go now, Geog, Biology and History all with the most learning. Biology is next and I am attacking that at the moment!!!!! I try not to think of geography because I honestly know nothing.
>
> Also we decided it would be rather nice to have a cake, not a birthday one but a choclate one layer, coffee t'other, butter icing inside, melted choc atop type! – would that be O.K.? Hope so, you could bring it down on One day event!!!!! I can't wait till then – you can boost my moralle après le Geographie horrifique!!! After that it is History, History, History – Freedom!
>
> Lots of love to everyone, all includes!
>
> Masses and Masses of love, hugs and kisses,
>
> Jen.

And here is another request of a rather more comprehensive kind.

> Dear Daddy,
>
> Thank you very much indeed for the lovely stamp, I am longing for Thursday week. I forgot to tell you at the beginning of term the porters and gardeners dug up two sculls and a lot of bones, when they were making an air-raid shelter and one is 30 yrs old & the other 2000 yrs old.
>
> In swimming I can go right under the water now, it is lovely.
>
> Do you mind if I tell you what I would like for my birthday, Sheath knife, money to get your violin mended, 1 pr of ballet shoes, 2/6d snowwhite book of easy music and pictures 'Snow White records' and

anything else any one would like to give me, and I would like some strawberries and sweets for my birthday.

With tons of love from
Anne

Another letter just asks for 'Shampoo, 3 coat hangers and a book of comic verse'.

One would hardly have cared to be a head of dorm or to have the nickname of 'Floorcloth'.

My Darling Mummy and Daddy,
    Wednesday it was Halloween and therefore there was great excitement in the dorms as everyone got ready various things to 'frighten' the head of dorm. Our dorm made some super ghosts which we hung over Floorcloth's bed, and then we put a most realistic dummy in her bed. She was so fumbly when she came in that it needed all our control not to laugh. And she really thought that we were asleep for she told the people outside that we were. Then she came back and was about to get into bed, gave a sigh, and then we all rose out of bed, wailing, ending in a shriek. Floorcloth said that she got quite a shock!

Parents are apt kindly to encourage their children's awakenings in the way of hospitable feelings.

Darling Mummy and Daddy,
    We have just had swimming – super! Lunch was quite decent. It was mince, and new potatoes and then a sort of blammonge (oops!) thing, you'll know what I mean. I have had to swop best friends as Jane had got fed up with me and so now I've got Helen. Nobody else likes her as she is a vegetarian and sometimes has to have special dishes and last week there were carrots for veg and Helen was given a huge pile and there weren't really enough for us. Everyone was

furious and made remarks. Miss Best saw us all frown-
ing at Helen and when lunch was over she sent Helen
out of the room and then gave us a great lecture about
learning to live with others however odd they were.
And when Miss Best had gone Helen came back and
everybody started pulling Helen's hair and Miss Best
unfortunately heard and came rushing in shouting
How dare you defy me and gave out order marks
gallore. Please can I bring Helen home for part of the
time? Her parents are sepparated. Just cabbage and
stuff like that. She has hay fever and always looks a
bit weepy. She's quite decent really. There is a film
tonight but we don't know what yet.

The following daring escapade reads like something from a
girls' school story except that in fiction one of the girls would
have turned out to be a non-swimmer and come near to
drowning.

The most important thing that has happened this week
is our midnight swim. The four of us who took part
were Mary-Jane (M-J), Anne, Sue Johnson and me.
We were going to do it on Wed. night, but for various
reasons it was delayed till Sat. night. At 1.30 a.m.,
M-J came and woke me. Then I went and woke Anne
and Sue. M-J and I then each took our swimming
costumes and crept downstairs. At the front door we
waited for Sue and Anna who arrived a few minutes
later. Then with quaking hearts Sue who was our
leader unbolted the door and turned the key. The noise
sounded terrific in the night, so we went into the
b——— and stayed quiet for about 5 minutes. Then
we decided to have another 'go' at the door. Sue opened
it and the others trooped out, and as I was bringing
up the rear I had to shut the door. In my nervousness
I let go of the handle and it made an awful clatter, but
eventually I did it. Then we slipped accross the grass.

The sky was very cloudy, but it was a warm night and we could see clearly. The long grass we walked through made what seemed to us to be a very loud noise. As we neared the pool 2 unearthly screeches rent the air. This very nearly made us want to give the whole thing up, but we finally satisfied ourselves that it was an owl. The noises at night are very frightening. Once up at the pool we changed quickly, and then slipped down the steps into the water which was lovely and warm. I was so panicky that I only swam a width, the others swam two widths. The ripples we made hit the side with loud 'smacks', then as iff to crown it the others started to giggle out of pure nervousness, so I had to force them to get out of the pool. We changed back into our pyjamas and put on extra jerseys. Then we summoned up courage and began the homeward trek. The way we went back struck us as being extremely funny because we were in full view of anyone who wanted to look out of the windows. I had forgotten to tell you that Clare had gone away for that night, and before she went she told us not to do anything peculiar or different in her absence!! We opened the front door and slipped the bolts and relocked it when we were inside. Then we went upstairs. Every board we stood on seemed to creek terribly. Once in the dorm we had to take the bolsters out of our beds. I was so excited that I just could not sleep for a long time afterwards! We had taken exactly half an hour on the whole thing!! *BUT* on Sunday morning Janet (our head of dorm) accused someone of walking about last night at about 2 o'clock. It was us but fortunately she did not seem to suspect us. We are now keeping our fingers and toes crossed that no one saw us.

Another thing I did was last Sunday. Jacki and I decided we did not want to go to evening service, so we went for a walk in the plantation. But we found that we had to spend all our time planning how to get back to the house without being suspected. So we eventually hid behind a tree outside the chapel, and then slipped in with the people coming out. We were quite convinced we had been seen but so far nothing has been said.

> Lots & Lots of Love,
> Joan Diane

However reassuring the letters attempt to be, parents know moments of acute anxiety.

Darling mummy and daddy,

how are you? I am very well here except for today we had lacrosse first thing, and I was just ready, and I began to swing on some bars in our cloakroom. Of course I fell off, head first, (dont worry) I fainted for about one minute then, the girls said, I started screaming a bit. The next thing I knew, I was in the San. with sister. I only spent the morning there. I have an enormous lump on the side of my head, I twisted my ankle, and bruised my knee. After that, I enjoyed myself as everyone started being kind to me. Earlier in the evening I had a splitting headache, but it was too late to go to surgery, so my pash (Victoria) gave me a disprin and I felt much better. Tiddily winks tail fell off but Victoria sewed it on again. Please, Please dont worry about me, I really am alright now. Next weekend my class and another one are going to Bristol Zoo. I shall write to Gran-Gran again and tell her. Thankyou for the stamps. By the way this paper is from Amanda Tanner who is a very nice older girl who sleeps next to me. Her arm is in plaster, but she is to have it off in 2 days.

> Lots of love
>
> Nicola

P.S. I love you. P.S.S. See you on my weekend out.

The liveliest, and the naughtiest for the last, with hopes (see the third paragraph) of more misbehaviour to come.

At the beginning of the term we had two new girls in my year. One was very plain and nice who found it difficult to adjust to our manners here. The other girl is American and brought with her from America two six-month-old snakes as pets. This girl was upstairs with seven others from my year when Vanessa, one of the seven, returned on the first day and heard that she might be sleeping in the same room with the snakes, she went totally white and refused very flatly. Her face dropped a mile and it looked as if she wanted to cry; it was a sight to see, very funny. On her first day the poor American found everyone keeping a good two feet away from her because of her snakes, she wore them round her neck, like necklaces. One is a python and the other a boarcontsricter (I think that is spelt wrong). When she first came they were about a foot-and-a-half long, but every time she feeds them they grow, which is once a week on a mouse each. She goes to the pet shop in the village and buys two mice and then when she gets back she feeds them. This means first stunning the mice by hitting them on a wall and then giving them to the snakes, who eat them whole. I will not say any more on the matter as it gets rather yucky!

Tonight at supper it was great, a riot! A large food fight began with bread and potatoes. To begin with it started round our table aimed at our friends, but once the master having supper with us got on to what was happening the food was aimed at him when he was not looking. He is a very odd looking man and is also very wet!! He is tall with an egg head with hair round the middle. It was such fun as he had no control at all. He threatened to keep us in the dinning-room until we had been quiet for five minutes, but that is impossible for us! Every time he turned round to walk away another ambush of rolls and hard-baked potatoes went for him. He got so angry he went red. Then everyone decided to run out so he screamed at us and we all rushed back. The head had to be summonned and a role called taken. The head went mad with us, screaming and saying how terrible it was. A lot of people got the giggles which made it worse.

Apart from these two things nothing has been happening here, no booze-ups or parties so far. I suppose there is hope yet.

How are you? I am very well and working extremely hard this term, much more than last. 'Is this possible?' you say. YES, well . . . I try my hardest.

9

Leisure

It is a moot point whether girls dressed up as boys look more improbable than boys dressed up as girls, but both such impersonations had to be resorted to in unisex boarding schools where amateur theatricals were a feature of the indoor and out-of-school activities: and a very popular feature too, is the general view. One school in particular showed admirable enterprise:

> Another very good idea which helped new girls to settle down was that they had to produce a play at the end of their first fortnight. Bussage was mad on acting and got up plays continually, culminating with a proper open-air entertainment for the parents in the summer term. This, of course, was right up my street, although it must have been an ordeal for people who didn't like acting. There were nine of us new girls my first term, an unusually large number for such a small school and we were all shapes and sizes from a baby of five to me, just fifteen. I took charge, naturally! I believe I am still remembered among the old girls for my bossy ways. I decided that we should perform our own – or rather my – version of *Beauty and the Beast*. Guess who had the fattest part? Me. I was the Beast, clad in a very smelly bearskin which adorned the wall in the Big Room. I wrote the script, I directed the show, and from then on Theatre dominated my thoughts. If I

hadn't been enjoying myself so much I should have
regretted RADA more than ever, but as it was I felt
my life on the stage was merely postponed, as indeed
it was.

In the following reminiscence, one rather wonders how the
flying episodes in the Darlings' nursery and elsewhere were
managed:

> Once a year we performed plays for Reverend Mother,
> the nuns and staff. I remember *Peter Pan*, *Quality Street*,
> *Charlie's Aunt* and quite enjoyable play readings –
> Masefield springs to mind.
>
> A very ambitious pageant was put on one early June.
> Many of the girls came from hunting circles so horses
> figured largely. My principal recollection is being a
> druid with a beard. It was a windy day and our beards
> took leave of our chins and formed haloes on our heads.
> Sharp thorns penetrated our thin sandals and sank
> into our feet, midges buzzed and the odd piercing sting
> made us wince. We had very little experience of rough
> living in woods apart from a really awful excursion
> as Girl Guides when we blundered through dense
> thickets, arranged a small fire and tried to poach
> eggs – the wet and tepid results were extraordinarily
> uninviting.

Ambition is as prevalent in the amateur theatre as in the
professional one:

> —I think I am definitely going to be a mariner in *The
> Tempest*, but I am only on in one scene and all I
> have to say is 'All lost, all lost!'
>
> —I longed desperately to play the lead in one of the
> school's dramatic productions, but I never got into
> the Big Time – *Berkeley Square* or *Joseph the Dreamer*,
> with tickets sold for cash to parents and anyone else
> who was willing to pay – except in the minor,

infilling, unimportant roles of slave or peasant or simply 'crowd'.

For *Joseph* they put me into suitably Biblical caftan, black wig and gold headband, balancing a vast tray of chocolate drops, cooked rice and peanuts on my head, which I had to offer Joseph's brethren whenever there was a lull in the action. Once at rehearsal, going on my rounds, I got too near the front of the stage and as the curtain came down, rather too rapidly for artistic effect, I was enfolded, tin tray and all; one of the lead weights caught me a glancing blow on the temple and I was knocked cold. The brethren thought it was hilarious and wanted to keep it in, but the Head ruled otherwise.

It was all right on the night of course, and it has to be said that my first entrance was impressive – the door at the back of the Hall was flung open and four of us, bier-carriers, appeared hefting a fairly heavy monarch all the way from Egypt to the Promised Land chanting on a single low-pitched note: 'Make way for Pharaoh, Way for Pharaoh Khyam, Lord of the Lords and Lord of the All Mighty, Make way for Pharaoh!' – to the banging of drums and cymbals and the dancing and prancing of slave maidens.

Since I actually Had A Part in this huge production, Mother nobly turned up, confidently expecting I would have at least one line of dialogue. She was to be disappointed in this, but she was so taken by surprise at my unexpected appearance from the *back* of the Hall, not to mention the comic sight I presented, blacked up with cocoa, that she hiccupped into hysterical laughter, swiftly converted the laugh into a cough, which in turn caused the Bishop (sitting in front of her) to pass her a lozenge and to whisper rather loudly, 'Do please control yourself, Madam!'

There were other, smaller productions, performed for internal consumption only, and in these I sometimes fared rather better – a Russian Prince in *Lady Precious Stream*, the lead in an all-singing all-dancing Western called *Bucking Jim*, and a witch in *Macbeth*. But I always thought it was a pity that Mother missed the German class performance of *Hansel and Gretel*, seen by only about fifty people of whom no more than six could have understood a word we were saying.

It is delightfully unusual to find a schoolgirl trying to master a chorus girl routine:

Of course out of school and holiday activities were extremely important to us, as glamorous occupations could then be sought unashamedly. Whenever I could, I went to communal tap-dancing classes given in a room over our local pub by Miss O'Shea. She was a toothsome charmer who must have only narrowly missed making it on the stage, and as well as 'tap' she taught us an admirable variety of precocious gestures. I still remember the zest with which we flung up our skinny thighs, high-kicking and parroting: 'If I had one wish to make (kick, kick – *SMILE*! – shuffle, tap, shuffle, tap) this is the wish I would choose . . .' (shuffle, tap, kick, kick – *SMILE!* etc.). I could never put my juvenile finger on what was missing, but I sensed that our performance somehow lacked the appeal of those leggy Hollywood lovelies whom we tried to imitate. This had something to do with the strange assortment of sizes and shapes in our chorus line: we ranged from the ages of eight to fourteen, from bird legs to busty splendour. Occasionally we rose to the heights of taking part in hastily put-together amateur shows in aid of local charities or the Spitfire Fund. Then, in the heady atmosphere of greasepaint and stage lighting, we chorusliners practised hatred against the 'star' of the troupe – a twelve-year-old privileged private-lesson taker who, in the borrowed glory of adult camiknickers, would don the inevitable 'Sweet Little Alice Blue Gown' and sing of its tender charms until hardly a Mum in the audience remained dry-eyed. There were always girls like this who, with undeniable charisma and plenty of opportunism, managed to hog the best parts in school drama productions. Mind you, being tall and having a rather powerful voice, I was lucky in the acting business; there were no boys in our orbit, and I often secured plum male parts (Drinkwater's Abraham Lincoln, for example).

Our cheery tap-*danseuse* goes on to relate an episode by no means unknown in wartime Britain, together with the rather rigorous application of a school rule.

Out-of-school activities also included occasional trips to London. This was then, according to my mother, full of iniquitous threats to schoolgirl safety – in the shape of young men in the uniforms of Free France, Free Poland and, most menacing of all, Free America! Until Uncle Sam entered the war for me and my school chums the American male was personified by Gary Cooper and Clark Gable. It was therefore disappointing to find that most of the friendly and ubiquitous GIs whom we came across at dances, on trains and in the cinema (but never at library lectures, cricket matches or tennis parties) bore no resemblance to our craggy Hollywood heroes. Bland in countenance, they were aptly dubbed 'Baby Faces' by many Londoners. Nevertheless their presence added vitality and zest to life, despite warnings from parents and teachers about what- happened- to- girls- who- went- to- Brighton-with-American-soldiers. (Why, I wondered, did it always have to be Brighton?)

It didn't always have to be Americans, however;

Canadians were just as spunky, as we learned from one of our Headmistress's dramatic morning prayer announcements. In the hols, apparently, two of our number had gone off in a lorry with a party of Canadian soldiers. (Gasp from assembled school!) As a result of this little joyride, one girl had become pregnant (even bigger gasp) and the other, as the Head so augustly put it, had got off 'scot-free'. It is to the Head's eternal credit that the name of the girl who'd simply had a good time was never revealed to us, though maternity absence for her companion prevented anonymity in that case. But, as so often happened at school, this liberality was soon to be counterbalanced by an extreme example of rigidity in the interpretation of a school rule. Eventually delivered of her offspring, the very young mother was allowed to return to the school to complete her studies for Matric. She wasn't exactly rebellious, though, understandably, the recent widening of her experience had made her a touch precocious. Caught one day powdering her nose in the cloakroom (and thus contravening an oft-reiterated rule) she was instantly expelled!

Dancing, with or without boys (or Canadian soldiers) provided a welcome break from work and games:

—During the two winter terms one evening a week we were taken to the ballroom of the Walpole Bay Hotel for a dancing lesson. We walked down at about seven in the evening and went past the hotels, where the lucky guests were just sitting down to dinner. It all looked very exotic to our eyes, with the waiters hovering over the guests, particularly as we had just partaken of a typical boarding school tea – plenty of it but not particularly inspiring.

—Saturday afternoons were a high point for some of the girls, for they were taken to a *thé dansant* at the Savoy Café in Prestatyn. About ten girls were allowed to go, travelling in a hired bus which at times seems to have had some difficulty in climbing the hills. The Savoy Café was divided into two parts, one for tea and one for dancing, with music provided by gramophone records. The school magazine records that on one occasion the visit of the Lowther girls afforded great entertainment to the people of Prestatyn, who gathered round the windows and peered in.

—In the Upper VI a party of us went to a dance at Marlborough; I recall being shown the classrooms by a spotty youth, but I don't think anything exciting happened. There was a return fixture, when a coachload of them came to a dance at our school; however the atmosphere was hardly conducive to romance, with the hall lights all on, staff sitting all round, orange squash to drink, a crowd of boys at one end and us at the other.

My friend Alison and I went to the garden sheds and had a secret smoke on the eve of her sixteenth birthday.

—Absolutely no contact with boys, youths, men was an edict most carefully impressed upon us. This was made more difficult by the proximity of a boys' College, but although they, on the whole, had fresh, eager faces and we reckoned they would be co-operative, if only given the chance, they remained forbidden fruit for many years. However, Coronation year proved too much even for British caution. The respective Headmaster and Headmistress met and took the plunge. We were to take part in the town Festival by dancing in public with the boys. The dances would be barn dances, folk dances, country dances. Exciting though this project was at first, in fact it afforded little scope for anything other than barn dances, folk dances and country dances. For, with the gaze of the public full upon us, it was all we could do to concentrate on the intricate twists and turns and high hops as favoured by the early English. To push into place our mute, hot-handed partners, who were somehow less quick at grasping the thing, occupied us fully. But the ice was broken and a further meeting of the sexes was to follow.

The following term the boys asked our forty best dancers to a dance in their gym. Ruthlessly they sent out their invitation at least six weeks in advance, causing a prolonged flutter among the chosen ones. There were, too, complications of a rare nature – problems which never before had the school come up against. What, for instance, should we wear? Being summer, especially ironed blue dresses, white ankle socks and gym shoes were eventually decided upon. Then, what should the boys wear? This problem was also turned over to our Headmistress. She summoned six of us to her sitting room to beat out a solution. 'I thought white open-necked shirts, shorts and gym shoes,' she suggested, 'and perhaps gay, different coloured sashes round their waists.' Our protests were of no avail. She would not even consider long trousers. Shorts for the boys it was.

The dance started awkwardly. Girls huddled at one end of the long, dusky gym, boys the other. The dancing master – 'the second best folk dancer in England' – (no riskier kind of dance was envisaged) stood on the stage, locking and unlocking his fingers and begging us through a microphone to mingle, mingle. Yet, despite the innocence of the dancing, the jellies in paper plates eaten on those long low benches that crouch by gym walls, the hesitant conversation and carefully reserved 'goodnights', the damage was done. For soon after this letters with the town's postmark began to arrive and were im-

mediately suspect. There were rumours about one
of Them being found in a coal hole with one of Us.
Headmaster and Headmistress were forced to call
another and less happy meeting – and so ended our
brief life with the boys.

—Once a year we had etiquette lessons. A very smart
woman appeared from the town dressed in a black
dress and pearls and we lined up in pairs and were
taught how to make introductions, how to curtsey
and how to be presented at court. I don't think
many of us ever were, but I still get nervous when
I introduce people.

We never met any boys and at twelve or thirteen
felt the lack. Brenda Stubbs, Madeleine Moffat and
myself formed a private club. We wore our Flanders
poppies long after Armistice Day as our club badge.
Our baptism of fire was to wink at the altar boys as
we went in or out of church. These were village boys
who served at Mass and at Benediction. They must
have thought it was Christmas every day of the
week. We were never caught. We got bolder. And
we were nearly expelled.

—The school had provided many wives for Empire
builders, but sex education had not progressed beyond the instruction to 'lie back and think of England'. Consider the restrictions surrounding the
annual school dance. For the rest of the year our
exeats were tightly scheduled to render contact with
the pink-cheeked wolves of the neighbouring boys'
College virtually impossible during term time. However, the less unruly members of the boys' school
were invited to the dance. For us, dress for the
occasion was formal white silk, with white stockings
(the latter only obtainable from the local under-
taker). Under this virginal garb we were compelled
to wear our baggy green gym bloomers. Imagine

the shapes! And at an age when the female form had its own unwelcome bumps and bulges. Liquid refreshment was in the form of a 'fruit cup'. For us, this was quantities of fruit juice to which a modicum of ginger beer was added. For the boys, ditto, but with the daring addition of cider. Should one, by mischance, obtain a glass of this intoxicating liquor, instructions were simple, 'Pour it into the nearest pot plant.'

Thirty years on I became friends with the daughter of a Singaporean merchant, who had attended the school in the late 1950s. In exchanging notes, I was amazed to learn the same performance was being repeated. The only improvement was that the bloomers had been replaced by figure-hugging gym shorts, which could be more adequately concealed beneath a 'Come Dancing' ball dress. The refreshments and instructions relating to them remained the same.

—Those Saturday dances! No men of course – just girls dancing with girls, girls dancing with staff, staff sometimes (from sheer boredom) dancing with each other – it all seemed a bit odd. I mean, parents paid to have us taught to foxtrot and waltz and quickstep, so perhaps it was all right to throw us together every Saturday, to try out our steps on each other – at least it gave us a chance to sit on the sidelines, to watch our particular crush, the girl we were 'on', as she took turns round the floor, to dare to hope for a dance with her ourselves.

—The school dance during the Christmas term was most popular (no boys of course) when we all took it in turn (by houses) to furnish the little 'sitting out' places round the sides of the Assembly Hall; they can only be described as igloos of eiderdowns, lit with torches covered with coloured paper to give subdued lighting, which in turn produced an atmosphere of secret calm where confidences could be exchanged.

A summer highlight for members of the sixth form was a visit to Glyndebourne or Covent Garden – all in evening dress, the only time apart from the school dance we were allowed to wear our 'own' clothes, although we became used to seeing the staff in evening dress as they wore it every night of the term for supper. The Headmistress always took us to the opera, wearing but everything – a fur stole, sequins, feather fan, kid gloves and her diamond rings on the *outside* of her kid-gloved hands! We were amazed, and a little embarrassed.

Leisure time was not always filled with activities as popular as dancing and acting.

—On Saturdays, everyone had to do her mending and, in those pre-nylon days, what a lot of mending there always was! For some strange disciplinary reason, this chore had to be done in total silence. No-one was allowed to speak a word until her mending was done, even if it stretched into the afternoon. When all was finished, there was one hour allowed for listening to gramophone records though no-one has left an account of what kind of music was considered suitable. One doubts if dance bands and crooners were acceptable. Girls using the Senior Common Room were judged capable of self-discipline but a matron or a teacher always sat with the Juniors. This was possibly a greater trial for the staff than the girls.

—Miss Holtaway taught needlework and every Friday afternoon white clothes were placed on the long tables and we all donned white sleeves and sat for two solid hours sewing. Each term every girl made

The Headmistress always took us to the opera, wearing but everything . . .

a garment and the needlework was really lovely. We did very fine darning in wool as well as linen and notchless button-holes. There was always a panic at the end of term about finishing the garments and no marks were given for uncompleted work. In my own day we had the same rule and one little girl made no effort and a little embroidered cloth went home half done. I quite forgot having found fault with the child but about five years later I received a small parcel and behold it was that little cloth, like 'bread upon the waters', returned 'after many days' and quite finished.

Considerable anxiety was everywhere displayed by school staffs as to what reading matter was suitable for the girls in their leisure time and some quite extraordinary prohibitions resulted. As regards the first one mentioned here, one can hardly imagine what the reactions of the authoress concerned would have been.

—I was one of the Assembly summoned to hear the High Mistress forbidding us to read any of Angela Brazil's books – if any found, instant burning; I have since wondered if she had any right to do such a thing, but it was 1920 and times have changed considerably since then.

—It was Miss Holtaway who covered all the library books in brown paper so that they were even more unattractive outside than inside. Some of them were marked 'S.S.' which signified 'Sunday Serious' and each girl was obliged to have one of these in hand for the silent hour on Sunday. Only one of the 'S.S.' books was popular. It gave a most vivid account of tortures inflicted on Christian martyrs! I could describe them now!

—Our reading was carefully vetted, so that no nasty modern novels would sully our infant minds.

Georgette Heyer was permitted, but smuggled copies of Ernest Raymond's *Tell England* or Warwick Deeping's *Sorrell and Son* were instantly confiscated. I found this particularly hard after being allowed to range freely through my father's library at home.

—After dinner we were all sent to lie on our beds, silently, for half an hour. We might read our library books – Matron held library sessions once a week; the books were gifts from past pupils, mostly, and were stored in a large bookcase in her room. We were never allowed a magazine or newspaper during the whole term. To have a magazine, or pack of cards, found in one's locker was a crime, penalty a conduct mark. Order marks, involving only one bread-and-butter tea, were for lesser crimes and they could be earned in hundreds of ways! All were totted up in the end of term reports for our parents to see . . . Good conduct, with high term and exam marks, earned a 'Starred Report', quite rare. One term I took 'Home' a starred report, quite inadvertently. I had been so unhappy, that I had sought solace in keeping my head down to work. That term I discovered Tennyson and saturated my mind in a volume of his poems. (Ever since, in times of sorrow, reading poetry has been my relief.)

—Our reading material was governed by the 'Index'; this was a list of prohibited books to be avoided at all costs by Catholic girls and it was read out to us in the Common Room, in hushed tones, from time to time. I remember on one occasion causing a *deathly* hush, when I announced that we had, at home, *Gone With the Wind* and several novels by Alexandre Dumas; it was suggested that I removed them discreetly from the shelves during the next holidays, for fear of them influencing my younger sisters.

Sometimes the luckier schools broke the term-time monotony with film shows, though here too censorship was important, and more difficult. And occasionally there would be a lecture or an outing or a picnic.

— Every so often we had a film on Sunday evenings, but, on many many occasions, I can remember not seeing all the film as the nun's hand shot over the projector when she realized that something unseemly was happening; once it was the birth of a sheep, another time, it was a young couple kissing, hardly that, they actually only 'pecked' each other. Sometimes we didn't know why the film was blacked out and spent the rest of the evening trying to imagine what it could possibly have been, we were so innocent.

— In my childhood electricity was little used. We had no electric light till we came to Bexhill and no telephone till we moved to St John's in 1910. Cinema shows were just coming in then, but with cracked and faulty films and machines which frequently went wrong. Music was supplied by some unfortunate female pounding on a piano and trying to keep up with the trotting horses in wild west scenes. 'Talkies' were nearly as bad at first. Very often the words did not keep pace with the actions. We never possessed anything but a silent cinema but the girls loved it as they could talk all the time themselves. We hired films about once a week and so Saturdays were quite gay. Now and then, towards the end, we hired a talking machine and film.

— If we were lucky, one of the day girls, who were in the minority and so greatly coveted for their hospitality, would invite us to share their home on a Saturday. We were allowed to go in our own clothes, regulations stipulated two 'non-uniform' dresses, and mine had been made specially by a lady with a grey moustache and cardigan to match. I preferred the red-spotted dress with the H-line waist to the black-and-white houndstooth check, but really anything was preferable to our ginger brown tunics, although we still had to wear brown knickers and lisle stockings when out on a visit. Small wonder we never came to any harm from the local youths or the nearby Army Recruits, whose barracks were enticingly placed next to our school and consequently were the subject of much speculation on our part!

Occasionally, films were shown on Saturday evenings, and to this day I cannot hear mention of *Mandy*, about the little deaf and dumb girl, without remembering the pent-up misery and distress unleashed by that particular tear-jerker. There were others, too, for whom tears were never far away, and for a while comradeship sprang up between myself and a timid half-Polish girl with an unpronounceable surname. She and I wept quietly in the underground cloakrooms before lessons each day, I, whenever I received letters from home, and she because letters rarely came. Her mother never appeared on our 'exit' weekends, and she was left virtually alone whilst the rest of us whizzed happily through the school gates to forty-eight hours of freedom. As I began to make friends my need for her diminished and I often wonder what became of that poor lonely child. I still recall her peaky, spectacled, tear-stained face, framed by wispy pigtails, waiting in vain for letters and parents who never arrived.

Friends were, then, finally made, my particular crony being Dorothy from Barnsley, who lived in the hope of one day meeting and marrying Nigel Patrick. She had more flair than most of us with the uniform, her sash just a little lower on the hips than permitted, a gold cross and chain escaping over the top of her blouse. Her mother was a nurse and sent back-copies of the *Nursing Times*; we gloated over photos of those with premature baldness and x-rays of cancer of the stomach. Under cover of darkness in the dormitory she inhaled on Woodbines, looking all of forty years old in a net covering her hair and cold cream thick upon her face.

—Monday evening concerts were our greatest terror. Everyone over fourteen had to play or recite and we all suffered agonies of nerves as we waited our turn to stand in the middle of the big hall, with the whole senior school sitting round with their 'work'. The Principal and her black spaniel sat at one end flanked by the prefects in high-backed leather chairs. It was always my great ambition to make her smile; I don't think she ever laughed. I chose poems by Walter de la Mare and I can still recite most of the adventures of the 'Old lady that went blackberry picking, along the hedges from Weep to Wicking' and what happened to the 'Three jolly farmers who once bet a pound each dance the other would off the ground'. There was one girl, whose grandfather was a well known playwright, who always recited in a very dramatic way. I remember 'Oriana, Oriana, Oriana' being repeated again and again with great feeling.

A professor came to lecture on Greek and Roman history. He swept in after the Principal trailing a very ragged gown, and every week he started by lifting his eyebrows and wrinkling his forehead into countless furrows, like the waves of the sea, and saying in a booming voice 'I told you but I dare say you've forgotten'; as there was no follow up or prep I dare say he was right. I now rather wish I had listened better.

Another charming old man, Professor de Sumichrast, gave us divinity lessons in the senior school.

He liked to be called 'Mr Sumi' and had us all in fits of laughter during break. 'Where are the British mentioned in the Bible?' he would ask. No one knew the answer. 'The meek shall inherit the earth,' he said and went off into peals of laughter. The British Empire was then at its height and as a European he found great amusement from his little joke, but there was no bitterness in him, he was a truly great Christian. I believe he was Polish. I carried on a correspondence with him after I left and used to go and see him and his wife.

In the winter terms the boredom of prep used to be relieved by visiting lecturers who told us about their travels and experiences, with the help of slides. Sir Francis Younghusband told us about his expedition to Tibet; he was the first European to enter the sacred city of Lhasa. Another day we were given a very exciting account of several British people who had been imprisoned by a Bedouin tribe, called the Senussi, in an underground chamber in the desert and how they were eventually rescued. A lecture on ants sticks in my memory and was a very worthy forerunner of David Attenborough's wonderful films of wild life. 'Evans of the Broke' was a very famous naval officer who told us the story of a naval battle in which his ship and HMS *Swift* destroyed six German destroyers. He had also been on the Antarctic expedition in 1909 and he took command when Scott died.

There was a lot of rustling and a strong smell of leather as Oski-non-ton came into the hall arrayed in all his finery as a Red Indian Chief. He told us about the Indian customs and actually made fire with a spindle, which caused great excitement and wonder.

—A glance through past copies of the school magazine gives an interesting glimpse of the social life of

Lowther College in the 1920s and 1930s. One of the highspots of the week was the Saturday evening entertainment, which took various forms. On the first Saturday of each term, Mrs Lindley held a dance and on succeeding Saturdays Whist Drives were held, recitations given, plays performed and special events held – for example, a Fancy Dress Dance in 1921 at which all dresses had to be made of paper. To give even further variety, Mrs Lindley engaged professional entertainers. In 1921 the school was entertained by Mr Uttridge, who gave an elocution recital, Mr Harold Scott, pianist (who was invited back because he was so popular), Mr Runnells Moss, who gave his celebrated rendering of 'A Christmas Carol', Mr Adrian Harley, who lectured on *Twelfth Night*, Miss Una Truman, pianist, and Madame Licette, a former pupil, 'that Prima Donna of such renown', who gave a vocal recital. In 1923 cinema shows were added to this selection of entertainments. The projector had to be kept near the doors of the gym when in use, so that it could be wheeled outside quickly when it caught fire. Unfortunately we do not know how often this occurred.

—There were, of course, periodical pleasant diversions: a course of lectures at the British Museum where white-haired bespectacled old gentlemen benignly led us, faint but pursuing, through the wonders of Antiquity, and there was the added thrill in archaeological experiment of writing one's name in the dust on the backside of a sphinx and hoping to find it there next week. There were expeditions to concerts and Shakespeare plays. There was the delight of Folk Song evenings round the grand piano in the Recreation Room, the jealously guarded retreat of Middle V, where Gracie Raikes, a staff as bonny as her voice was enchanting, would hold us spell-bound for an hour with an endless repertoire from 'Blow Away the Morning Dew' and 'As I Was A-Walking', to 'The Coventry Carol' and 'The Christ-child Legend'.

But the cream, the jewel, the Mecca, of the year's outings was the Naval and Military Tournament at Olympia. There went the whole school, its bosom expanding with jingo passion, its whole soul swooning with the love of every nice girl for sailors and soldiers indiscriminately.

On one sad occasion, during the morning before this heart-throbbing afternoon, I had inadvertently twirled a pirouette of sheer boredom in singing-class, and 'Pa' [Mr Evetts], his baton raised for a melodious choral fanfare, perceived its naked unashamedness. Crashing from his dais, he descended on me breathing outraged fire and smoke, and bade me report myself instantly for unbridled insolence to the 'Lady-Principal'. Wise in my generation, however, I postponed this inauspicious interview until the evening.

'And why did you not come to me at once?' enquired Miss England, 'as it was naturally assumed you would be obedient and honourable enough to do?'

'Because,' I said simply, 'I knew you would not let me go to the Military Tournament, Miss England.'

'And certainly you were right! How *could* I have allowed such a rude little girl to go? You will make a suitable apology for your disgraceful behaviour in the singing class; and I am disappointed in you, Barbara, that you were dishonourable.'

But I think that was one of the times when her hooded eyes twinkled, for after all I had solved a problem for her.

—Guiding at school offered many delights. There was the genuine interest of all the things one had to learn in order to Be Prepared, and I found I had a gift for Signalling. The same Philty Baba of the riding party and I became the school's crack pair both in semaphore and morse, and even snatched the prize from among thousands at a huge Rally in Hyde Park, at which Princess Mary, still in the flush of girlhood with her exquisite complexion, was the queen-bee Commissioner. She had given gracious permission for us to keep our dark green and gold school uniform instead of adopting the traditional navy blue, and – for we were a smart and pretty troop – we stood out among the others in a most gratifying manner. I seem to remember the message with which Philty Baba and I won our laurels was: 'In an emergency a baby's cradle may be satisfactorily arranged in a laundry-basket!'

But the surpassing joy of the whole year was our fortnight's camping on a remote part of the Sussex Downs. We occupied an old Elizabethan barn across a wide farmyard from a mellowed farmhouse with the kindest host and hostess in the world. They had two little boys who progressed solemnly from year to year as 'Mr Two' and 'Mr Three', 'Mr Three' and 'Mr Four', and so on. The camp was not unduly formal; we nailed our company colours and the union jack to the barn door on arrival, lined up before them, gave them a perfunctory salute and forgot all about them until it was time to pack them up and take them home again.

We were there to enjoy ourselves – and enjoy ourselves we did. Shorts were of course unheard-of for girls, but bloomers and jerseys were a free and easy outfit in which we even dared as far as Littlehampton for bathing picnics. The three staff in charge were charismatic leaders and extremely High Church, and as the two nearest 'little lost Down churches' had celibate twin-brothers as rectors –

as light in heart as they were heavy in ritual – we were adopted as their family and they arranged for us exciting programmes of exploration, outings and cricket-matches.

As regards picnics, I have to report receiving verbal information from a lady who wishes to be anonymous. She states that at the age of twelve she composed what she considered to be a side-splitting riddle. It ran, 'What do people do on a picnic?' and the answer was 'They pick their knickers.' At the next school picnic she proudly trotted out this mild indecency, was overheard by the Headmistress, sent instantly home and very nearly expelled.

—At Godolphin, Ascension Day was a holiday – at least, it was for the fortunate day girls. We boarders had to play Tip and Run in the morning (what a *treat*) and in the afternoon we had to go in a fleet of coaches to some beauty spot for a picnic (Grovely Woods stands out in my memory) and there spoil (or make) the afternoon for any innocent travellers who happened to be abroad. I do recall a man cycling along one of the tracks when all two hundred of us (clad all in white Aertex shirts, navy divided skirts, four inches above the knee when kneeling, navy socks and brown lace-ups) stood up to sing the Doxology before tucking into our sandwich, fruit slab and apple; the poor fellow fell off in amazement and most of us praised Father, Son and Holy Ghost in gales of laughter. When we arrived back at school we all trooped into the Hall for prayers and 'Hail Thee, Festival Day'.

Princess Margaret's wedding day was another holiday; after another thrilling morning's Tip and Run we were taken to Barton-on-Sea, where we sat on an extremely stony beach and shivered in the wind.

—But there were happy days at Sedbergh. It was a
beautiful spot, in the heart of the Pennines, with
their shallow, stony, sometimes treacherous, rivers.
In the summer sometimes, Saturday picnics were
arranged. We walked to a riverside, carrying two
huge, black, iron kettles and baskets of bread and
butter. For a short time we were freed from walking
in crocodile. We scattered along the river bank
gathering sticks and lit fires on the stones, to boil
the kettles to brew smoky tea. We were allowed to
remove our stockings and paddle. Those limestone
river banks were like gardens, with wild flowers,
and crowded with nests of sand martens and dip-
pers, and once I even found a kingfisher flashing
into a secret hole. Also, very occasionally, wagon-
ettes from the White Hart were hired and we went
out for the whole day, usually to visit one of the
well-known underground caves. On the day of King
George V's coronation, we had lunch at a small inn
at Barbon, sitting at trestle tables in a barn, where
we enjoyed new bread, with country cheese, and
cider (all at fourpence a head) and with a warm
welcome. These 'Extras' were duly recorded on our
end of term accounts, along with dancing and music
lessons, and overcharges on laundry. There would
also be a record of medicines, like my malt and cod
liver oil, fruit salts etc. We were so happy on these
outings, we sang all the way home, until the wagon-
ettes passed through the big gate. It was always a
silent party that drew up at the side door. Literally
we never passed out of that gate, or crossed the
boundary of the plantation, except in an escorted
crocodile, once, during the whole twelve-week term.
A conduct mark was the minimum punishment for
infringement of this rule.

—Miss Beale, as well as being in charge of the cash,
was also in charge of our sewing and our social

behaviour. Twice a week we went down to the drawing-room, which was her domain, and sat around the fire while she read aloud to us. She was a wonderful reader and we enjoyed these occasions enormously, especially the weekday period when we took our sewing with us and she read Dickens. On Sundays we were not allowed to sew and the books were always about martyrs, which wasn't so good, but the fire was still lovely and those hours in the drawing-room were about the only time in the winter terms when I really felt warm.

As well as the readings we had whist parties. This was to teach us manners and polite conversation. Half of us were told off to be gentlemen, and as I always seemed to be one of those I never really learnt how to be a lady. On the credit side, however, I am never at a loss for conversation.

10

Crushes

Romance now rears its head shyly and pretty innocently in the shape of the 'crush', the 'pash', the 'having a thing about'. No instances of actual sexual involvement are reported or anything even vaguely physical. A horrified revulsion might well have been the result of amatory dilly-dallyings, for these affairs were on an altogether higher plane, a plane where a look, a smile, a kind word were all that were required or expected and were quite sufficient to keep the fires blazing. Interestingly, and inversely from the customary and difficult complications in boys' schools, the crush seems to work one way only and from, usually, a fourteen-year-old who has become besotted with the hockey captain or the head girl or the games mistress. Instances of senior girls going 'soppy' and making eyes at an attractive little new girl are non-existent, though I dare say that when the seniors found themselves admired, some did not discourage the adulation and may well have been happy to encourage it.

There was a Titian-haired prefect for whom I swooned with love during the whole of my first year, 'A daughter of the Gods divinely tall and most divinely fair'. I wrote poems to her, and remember one was about cheese which she had made me eat at supper. I had told her how it revolted my whole being and she had riposted very gently that that was a pity because it was an outsize Wensleydale which her father had presented to Miss England to help feed the school; on another occasion he sent venison, which was loudly acclaimed. Food was hard to come by in those war years, and young people's needs were not put forward as they have been since; bacon and cabbage appeared frequently on our menu and we chewed it philosophically in our stride.

Then the divinity left and my hungry questing heart, starved of suitable fodder at home, throve on those friendships which have ripened through the years, bearing blossoms and fruit of a sweetness beyond compare.

But before this particular divinity actually left, poetry recitations provided an excuse for a thrilling encounter. At this school each girl was expected to be able to perform in public.

As I could neither sing nor play, I had *faute de mieux* to recite, and found myself among a happy band of such second-rate performers. There was Hope, who gave a dramatic rendering of 'The Highwayman' so many times, as a dare, that even Miss England showed signs of having *heard* it somewhere before; so Hope cunningly intermingled it with 'Is there anybody there? said the Traveller' for the rest of her years at school. But I was conscientious and really strove to give pleasure, and to this end I acquired quite a wide repertoire. One of my earliest treasures was Byron's 'Isles of Greece', but in the penultimate verse there was an immodest line which worried me. Should I say it? I felt far better *not*, but I would seek advice. From whom? Ah! the Titian-haired divinity (it was during my first year) would guide me along this slippery path; and also it would be an excellent and legitimate excuse for approaching her, for she did not encourage starry-eyed pursuit.

Trembling deliciously, I went upstairs and knocked timidly at the Library door. A sub-prefect opened it.

'Please,' I said, 'Can – may – I speak to Violet?'

The divinity appeared and, pink and diffident, I told her of my problem.

'Which is the line?' she asked. I handed her the book. 'There!' I showed her.

'*Where?*' she said. '*There!*' Again I pointed.

'I don't see it,' she said, poker-faced. 'Just say it to me.'

Suffused with blushes, I mumbled, 'To-think-such-breasts-must-suckle-slaves!'

'Well,' she said crisply, 'It's a long poem, so why not just leave that verse out? No one will notice.' And she went back into the Library and shut the door, while I lingered a little lost in bliss. Only years later, when I was a prefect myself, did I appreciate the sudden shout of laughter from within, which pursued me along the passage, and even trailed me down the stairs.

A Hampshire contributor gives a good over-all picture of the 'pash' and other matters.

Being 'on' somebody had no sinister connotations, bore no relation to the lopsided love affairs which, I am told, go on in boys' schools – far from it. If the object of affection hove over the horizon, there would be a mad scurry for cover, lest she smile, stop and talk, even – heaven forbid – ask one to run an errand! Honestly – one nearly died! And it was such a relief to escape from the magic aura to the safety of the lockers in the Library Corridor where one kept concealed the trophies of one's adoration – the hair ribbon, the tennis ball she used at the last big match, the snapshot taken from behind the laurel hedge. There was only one thing worse than the agonies of being 'on' someone,

and that was growing up and becoming the object of
a snivelling junior's affection – by then it all seemed
SO SILLY.

The Head was very keen to instil healthy thoughts
in healthy minds and she saw to it that we started with
healthy bodies. We started the day out on the playing
fields, running about with 'lax' sticks in hand, jumping
hurdles, practising our serves and backhands. If the
weather were unkind there was no escape – it was a
matter of 'off gym slips and ties' and a quick lollop
along the seafront and back. Developing bosoms in
inadequate Kestos bras bumped merrily in time to our
footsteps, blue bloomers gradually parted company
with brown woollen stockings, the gap between becoming wider and pinker the nearer we got to home. No
need to warn us not to talk to nasty strangers – no
nasty strangers would have fancied us.

Some of the College boys did, though – in dark blue
blazer and straw boater, two by two, their 'croc' would
pass our 'croc' on the promenade each Sunday and
blushing, we'd exchange furtive smiles and giggles,
little enough in itself, but sufficient to titillate our
awakening senses. We only actually MET them, were
actually allowed to SPEAK to them when we gathered
at the College for music and drama competitions.
Then, discipline relaxed, we could have mingled, but
when the mind is totally occupied with:

> Once when Peboam the winter
> Roofed with ice the big sea water . . .

mere boys fall back into obscurity. In any case, we
discovered, boys in the mass are smelly – and we'd
gather up our metaphorical petticoats and concentrate
on Hiawatha.

From long ago and far away there comes an instance of an
innocence that, one feels, can exist no more.

No need to warn us not to talk to nasty strangers – no nasty stranger would have fancied us.

Incidentally, sex was never mentioned in all the time that I was there and as far as I was concerned the facts of life were never discussed and we never knew when the girls in one's bedroom were menstruating, although we lived in such close proximity. Were we odd or was it the environment? We were amazingly innocent in those days and it simply did not occur to us. One's personal things were private to oneself and not to be discussed.

Cases are rare in which sexual ignorance or, as here, actual sexual abhorrence and discouragement did much harm.

In that all-female society, we were subject to strange 'Pashes'. There was a cult to declare oneself devoted to a member of staff, or another girl. Our Headmistress encouraged the belief that sex was filthy, and the very thought or mention of it was degrading, praising the love between David and Jonathan above all. Marriage was a last resort for the lower orders and more stupid people. Girls were educated in this atmosphere of isolation and loneliness and the lonely staff members also developed their intense affairs. Some of the older and more sophisticated girls understood what it all meant, and there were groups of giggling and jeering friends. But at twelve years old, I did not have a clue.

It is delightful to find such store set by ordinary friendships and that friends were often weighed and measured and graded, like eggs. And a new interpretation appears of the initials B.F.

We had 'crushes' on each other – my mother at the Convent many years earlier called them 'pashes' – when you were small you had a crush on either a prefect, the head girl, or the games' captain, (or even a nun). When I arrived at the top of the school I found that small girls had crushes on me. We also had V.B.F's and B.F's – 'very best friends' and 'best friends', there was a subtle difference. We were able to purchase at a piety stall on Sunday mornings for 1d or 2d each a 'Holy Picture', a small picture of a saint or the B.V.M., which were used to mark pages in our missals; these were used as birthday cards over and over again, we would cross out the message to us and overwrite it with one to the next 'birthday girl' and so on. BUT they were also used to write messages or requests on – 'Darling Angela, please, please will you be my V.B.F.? Pat says she won't be my V.B.F. any more, only my B.F. I MUST have a V.B.F. SO PLEASE be mine . . . lots of love and kisses etc.' Then a holy picture would come back – 'Darling Verney, Of course I will be your V.B.F., but first I must tell Rosalie that I cannot be hers any more . . . loads of love and kisses and hugs etc.'

I don't really know even now if any of these crushes or friendships had lesbian overtones – we certainly knew nothing of that specifically. When I was sixteen I became very friendly with a Spanish girl who came to the school; we became V.B.F.'s and to this day are still friends and exchange our children during the summer holidays etc. In those days, however, I can remember creeping out of my room in the middle of the night and visiting her in her bed in her room, where we used to lie close together and talk; I enjoyed these visits, but don't really recall having any particular sexual feelings.

On the rare occasions when there was animosity between girls, a rather frightening picture presents itself.

Among the new girls at the start of the summer term was one called Mona. She was in the Lower IV, like myself, and a month older. It was a late age to start at school and on the first night of term after Prayers Miss Wilson sent all the new girls from the room and addressed us. Mona, she told us, had been taken away

from her last school because she had been so teased
for being fat, therefore, on no account were we to
comment on her appearance. It hadn't struck me that
she was fat – a trifle thick-set, perhaps, with a slightly
curved nose and pretty dark wavy hair.

There was a general feeling of sympathy for Mona.
Miss Wilson at once put her on to ryvita at all bread
meals. She did not, however, lose weight and Miss
Wilson soon discovered that she had been helping
herself to bread and butter, though how she achieved
this under so many watchful eyes was a mystery. She
was immediately labelled a Tyke (with Miss Wilson,
'Tykes' were bad and 'Lambies' were good) and
accused of being thoroughly slippery.

Mona and I never got on together, our personalities
clashed, but I remember on one occasion feeling
thoroughly sorry for her. Mona had been caught out
in a lie and was 'A nasty piece of work'. A school
meeting had been summoned and Miss Wilson said
that in consequence of Mona's lie the whole school
must suffer and therefore every conceivable privilege
would be withdrawn. This said, she stormed from the
room, calling over her shoulder, 'I leave Mona to the
mercy of the school.'

The door closed behind her, and as it did so there
was a brief hush like the moment before a wave breaks
and ended like the baying of wolves and everyone
(except Prue and I who stood shocked and weak at the
knees) hurled themselves at Mona and dragged her off
the chair on which she had been sitting. I can still
recall the sick feeling at the pit of my stomach.

Even if the average girl was, during the holidays, friendly with
a boy, she seems swiftly to have forgotten him during term.

We were very innocent about sex. Some girls used to
get 'pashes' on older girls, but all it amounted to was

gazing at them in chapel and writing notes to tell them how wonderful they were. I do remember a rumour that the girls at one school were not allowed hairbrushes with handles, and although we all laughed knowingly at this, we did not discuss with each other what the reason might be. We never saw any men, except the odd job man, who was fat, with blackheads on his nose, our Headmaster/priest, a man who taught us national dancing, and a pianist called Raymond, whom we all dubbed weedy and feeble (our most damning insult). Although we were mostly attractive girls, training for a career on the stage and going to parties in the holidays, we didn't miss the opposite sex. I was eighteen when I left and never wished that we were co-ed. In my time there were two older girls who were rumoured to have 'done it', but we never knew for sure.

There are, however, exceptions to every rule. Here is a schoolgirl who found life intolerable without male companionship and thereby achieved a pattern of naughtiness that it would be difficult to equal (her mother also gets 0 out of 10 for behaviour).

At school, and being so unhappy, the only comfort I had was when the workmen came to mend the attic roof (which was out of bounds). I used to sit and smoke with them and talk my miseries out. When I was caught doing this, I was put into a dormitory with the head girl and a prefect. That first term the girls sent me to Coventry and stole my tuck.

At this horrid school on Saturday and Sunday afternoons I used to have to go for a walk in a croc and I would get at the end of the croc and then slip away into Marston and meet two young mechanics and ride around in customers' large cars. But one day we were caught red-handed by the school matron who was in the Headmistress's car and taking a sick child to hospital. And there I was sitting in the back of the borrowed car and elegantly smoking a cigarette. That evening I was expelled. To save the embarrassment of my parents coming to fetch me the next day, I slunk away across the fields for miles and caught a bus to the nearest station and got a train to Paddington. When, after many hours, I arrived home, which was on Wimbledon Common, my mother handed me a large glass of brandy!

11

Health

Physical fitness has always been a matter of extreme importance and in the first decades of the century boarding schools were greatly assisted and enlightened by a helpful volume called *Health at School*. Though it brought messages for both sexes, it was the work of the 'resident physician' (school doctor) of Rugby School and was possibly inspired, if that be the verb, by the horrifying outbreak of typhoid fever at a famous public school which resulted in numerous deaths, the temporary closing of the school, and the necessity to rethink entirely the school's antiquated drainage system.

The good doctor's name was Clement Dukes, his book was dedicated to dear old dead Arnold and nowadays it makes jolly reading as a period piece. Useful illustrations and charts abound – 'Archer's Water-tight Sewer Pipe'; 'How to Sit at the Pianoforte' (no slumping or slouching); 'A School Grease-trap in Operation'; and 'Average Heights and Weights of the Most Favoured Classes' – classes in this case meaning divisions in society rather than the Classical Sixth – a comparison between these favoured persons and the 'Artisan' class showing the latter, surprise, surprise, to be somewhat shorter and lighter. Dr Dukes omits nothing although information on how at Rugby they resuscitate drowning boys, together with the mortality rate from measles, hardly inspires confidence in parents.

Never mind, for there are handy tips aplenty. A child with gouty parents should have a hilltop school facing south and planted firmly on gravel (even nowadays gravel seems to be the ideal thing to aim at). Rheumaticky children should beware of clay. Where there is any insanity in the family, avoid all cramming for exams. Demand from the Headmaster or Headmistress full details of her subsoil drainage, her water levels and her proximity to an alluvial plain (*not* recommended). In the case of boys, is the Matron elderly? Is it realized, again in the case of boys, what hot baths *at night* may lead to? And finally has the school been sufficiently sensible to install (and if not why not?) one of the new earth closets 'as suggested and devised by the Rev. Henry Moule', presumably during an extended leave of absence from altar, pulpit and font?

In adult life the question 'Have you been?' refers more often than not to something agreeable – the Turner exhibition or the latest Ayckbourn play – but in the schools of today and yesterday it is the accepted way of enquiring about the success, or not, of bowel movements.

After breakfast, those who had not previously been to the 'boo' as we called it, were dispatched to the six house lavatories, known as Front 1 and 2, Buckingham Palace, Top 1 and 2 and the Little Cloakroom. Front 1 and 2 were adjacent and the most salubrious; they were small and light and above the front door porch. The window behind each seat was covered with a rather parchmenty patterned paper on which shapes and initials could be scratched with a tie pin or hair slide to while away the time. You could also converse in whispers with the fellow sufferer on the other side of the wooden partition. Buck Pal was on the same landing opposite the back stairs; it was also a bathroom and very cold. The Little Cloakroom was a small panelled room with a minute window, so dark that even with her torch there was a chance that Miss Williams would think one had performed better than was in fact the case.

Except for those fortunate ones blessed with a quick let down, we were doomed to sit for ten minutes. At the time it seemed eternity. Then if something had been produced you wrote your initials in white chalk on the lid. After this, quaking a little at the knees, you made your way to Miss Williams' bedroom and knocking on the door announced, 'Please, Miss Williams, it's Jane (or Ann or Margaret), I've been very well.' (Very unlikely.) 'Quite well.' (Barely possible, unless previously dosed with syrup of figs and paraffin.) To any of these she would say 'Pull it' if the girl was known to be regular and trustworthy, or to unfortunates like me she would say, 'Leave it and try again later.' Other grades were 'fairly well,' which might or might not rate 'Try again later,' or might involve one being sent back for another ten minutes there and then, along with 'Badly' and 'Very badly' and 'Please Miss Williams, I can't go!'

A feature of the school was that in winter there were great jugs of cabbage water, dark, strong-smelling and salty. It was served in the Little Prep Room, midmorning, while we were doing our obligatory ten minutes hair brushing. All those who were irregular at the boo were expected to down a glass for the good of their bowels.

It was a girl called George who taught me a simple method of partially opening the bowels. Each washstand had upon it a jar of common salt, and with a handful of this in cold water we were expected to gargle night and morning. George suggested I drink the morning gargle as she did. Probably by autosuggestion it worked to the extent that I was now quite frequently able to report to Miss Williams that I had been 'Fairly well.'

In winter there were great jugs of cabbage water, dark, strong-smelling and salty, served in the Little Prep Room.

An altogether less rigorous anti-constipation routine was favoured by a Headmistress with a charmingly original approach.

> The Principal, a Miss Nugent-Thorpe, took the 'little 'uns' (like myself, aged eight) under her wing in a very real way. She insisted on us calling her 'Auntie'. To make up for the lack of maternal love, Auntie invited us to join her in her giant-sized bed each morning. We all gathered in her bedroom, at the door of which stood a bucketful of apples. She passionately believed these to be a guaranteed preventative against sluggish bowels! We all made a beeline for the foot of the bed to avoid having to sit beside this good intentioned lady who then read to us while we silently or, rather, not so silently, munched our apples, at the same time playing football under the bedclothes with the cold stone pig which had made its way to the bottom of the bed. Auntie really enjoyed this halfhour and industriously sat knitting, while reading, with her needles carefully wedged into her armpits. Marilda, her off-white poodle, who permanently smelt of Blue Grass toilet water, more often than not joined us in the morning ritual in bed!
>
> After breakfast, Auntie, ever concerned about 'motions' insisted that the 'little 'uns' sat on potties in the dormitory until their business was done. My sister recollects how the older girls used to rush down the corridor clutching their noses for the fearful pong that emanated from the dormitory. One memorable occasion I was left, forgotten, for one and a half hours as I had been unable to produce anything bigger than a peanut and when I got up in tears immediately collapsed on the floor in a heap because my limbs had gone to sleep!

But elsewhere we find no confidence at all in the widely-held belief that an apple a day keeps the doctor away. And once more, in adult life, 'Marjorie has had an accident' means that she has been run over by a lorry. Not so in scholastic circles.

Two of my most vivid memories are of being forced to drink a glass of revolting senna pods in the evening and of being locked in one of the enormous and numerous toilets the next morning, expected to produce results from the odious drink of the previous night. The emphasis on this function was quite astonishing and the overriding feelings of fear and guilt should there be failure were quite terrifying and resulted in a short sharp smack on the bare buttocks by Matron.

My second memory in this connection was of being left for about three hours in one particular toilet which was unfamiliar to me, simply because I had been forgotten and was far too terrified to move without permission.

I also remember, vividly, standing in the hall for Assembly while the Lords Prayer was being recited and having a sudden and uncontrollable urge to pass water. Needless to say I did not make it and the resultant puddle on the polished floor turned me into the most loathsome creature in the school, to be treated with the utmost disdain. I was sent to the kitchens to get a cloth to clear up, where I was promptly kicked on the backside and sent sprawling by a member of the kitchen staff; my humiliation was overwhelming and complete.

And on and on the sad revelations roll . . .

Unfortunately she had another source of power over me. As our dormitory mistress, it was her duty to inspect our tongues at intervals, and send the owner of a furred tongue to Matron for a dose, choice of cascara, or liquorice. Every time I was caught with a 'filthy' tongue. This was quite a disaster for me, because most of the time, I was plagued with a form of diarrhoea and the generous dosing resulted in urgent requests to be excused for yet another trip to that row of draughty WCs. Then, at half-term weigh-in, it was found that I had lost seven pounds in six weeks. So as we marched out of the dining-room next time I was stopped by Matron, who told me I was to have malt and cod liver oil after each meal. But I never saw the doctor, who held his clinic in Matron's room every Tuesday. Anyway he was a doddering old man and the cause of much hilarity amongst the few girls paraded before him, who swore he gazed down their throats, tapped their knees, and gave Matron a bottle of pink medicine for the patient. My tormentor's final effort was to bring me a glass of Eno's fruit salts every morning to 'restore my appetite'!

It is very rare to fine juvenile defecation treated in a carefree and offhand manner and so this Hampshire example comes as a refreshment.

My parents weren't very happy about my school (I was fifteen). It was pretty old-fashioned and severe and of course one was all the time 'on one's honour' to do this or that and one of the things we had to own up to was success or failure in the Lavatory Stakes. Every morning a mistress appeared at Prayers (it was assumed that by then you had 'been') with a large ledger, known to us as 'The Bog Book', and we had to report results – very lowering and awful and embarrassing. It made one actually afraid to use the lavatory, so great were our fears of a nil return.

Anyway, my mother heard splendid reports of a school near Winchester and so I was transferred. My new school's Headmistress was a Miss Forrester – very pretty and quite young – and I assumed that one had to own up to the usual and as no ledger appeared on my first morning I knocked at the Head's door and went in and just said, 'Please, Miss Forrester, I've been.' 'Been where?' she said. 'To the lavatory.' 'Oh my goodness,' she said, 'we don't have any of that shame-making rubbish here. Just go when you can and be glad of it. Nobody wants to hear about it. We think all that reporting stuff is a bit common and vulgar. Of course, if you haven't been to the lavatory for three or four days, you'd better go and tell Matron. But you're a free agent.' I could have hugged her.

It was a remarkable school for there never seemed to be any punishments. It was quite enough just to know that Miss Forrester disapproved of something you'd done. It was rumoured that she had once come upon a group of senior girls smoking, puffing away and thinking themselves fearfully grown-up, and she just gave a loud laugh and said, 'I really cannot tell you how fearfully silly you all look.' It put them off for ever.

Routine physical check-ups were never popular.

On returning to school after the holidays, we were subjected to a vigorous health inspection. This was *not* a very flattering reflection on our homes. First our hair was scraped through for nits and until we had 'stripped to the waist with shoes and socks off' and been examined, we were not considered worthy to be accepted back into the fold.

Our housematron, Miss Frost, had a booming voice and after she had looked us over she would bellow 'Feet!' This command meant turning your half-naked body through 180° and first lifting one foot and then the other to her inevitable question, 'Any warts, corns or verrucas?' You trembled as she peered at these offending feet and dreaded that she might find little telltale symptoms of these three scourges which would lead to hours in the sanatorium or, at most, amputation of the offending foot.

After years of these three recognised dastardly foot complaints, there arrived another on the scene, namely Athlete's Foot. You were required to stand to attention whilst the dreaded Miss Frost would kneel down and violently pull your toes apart one by one. This meant that there was no way to hide the fearful fungus because as your toes were pulled apart, the splits (which had nearly healed) would be torn open again, revealing the all-too-obvious red gash glaring forth and a muffled scream would come from your mouth.

When we were *really* ill, as opposed to 'making a fuss', 'needing extra hankies' or 'needing a dose of phenolphthalein to open the bowels' we were sent to Surgery. This was a sterile bleak room near the kitchen where two formidable uniformed nursing sisters presided. Sister Naylor was fearsome with white hair, rimless glasses, no humour and a tall thin towering body. We put her at about aged eighty. The other, Sister Cooper was rather stout, stern and starchy, but was unique in her eagerness to titillate our minds with 'the outside world' and not being an actual teacher and not having been at the school *too* long, we found her very daring and exciting.

At girls' schools, and as now in life, female hair, and what to do for the best with it, is a constant problem and preoccupation.

Keeping our hair clean was another hygienic problem for us teenage girls. It was considered to be bad for our health to wash the hair too often. We were allowed to wash it every month which seemed like an eternity as the hair became more and more greasy and unsavoury smelling.

Nature was once again allowed to take its course and the 'natural oil', as the grease was euphemistically called, was to be revered. As our scalps began to itch we would shake tins of talcum powder over our heads and rub the powder into the scalp. Then we would brush our hair to rid ourselves of the signs of this sinful practice of abolishing nature's bounty.

Interestingly enough it was practically unheard of for any of our dirty heads to be hosts to parasites. They obviously didn't fancy us much either.

There were a few girls whose hair was dry and they would hold Dandruff Competitions, sitting in chairs with heads held forward over their laps. At the starting signal, they would scratch and scrabble their nails through their hair, dislodging the flakes and periodically wafting their hands over the tangled mass to encourage the showering blossom to flutter down. This smothered their beautiful royal blue dresses with a veritable snow storm. The winner with the biggest lapful of dandruff was very highly regarded and very much envied by those with greasy locks who were unable to produce such wondrous effects.

And hair of another sort could make difficulties.

Another distressing sign of puberty was under-arm hair and it was totally banned to remove this. Nature again was not to be tampered with and if Nature was good enough to enrich our armpits with fuzzy hoary locks, then we were to be grateful for such munificence. One term, one of my friends smuggled into school a pretty, pink razor designed for ladies. It bore the name of Nymph and on the blade packet there was a shapely, hairless goddess. Seven of us huddled into a locked bathroom and there in turn we scraped and tore at our armpits, passing the glorious implement from one to another until all the blades were blunt and all the offending armpits sore, scarlet, blood-tinged but best of all HAIRLESS – what joy!

With all these hygienic horrors abounding it is obvious that the most devastating of all were periods. Since the whole subject was regarded as shameful, humiliating, and offending against propriety, modesty and decency it was never discussed.

All dates of periods had to be kept in Matron's Black Book and after shoe-cleaning duties we were invited to enter our dates in appropriate pages and columns. We were only too pleased to do this because we knew that if we had no dates and had kissed one of our brother's friends in the hols, we must be pregnant. We weren't quite sure how the two things were related, but it was worth making up fictitious dates to enter in the book in order to ward away the evils of pregnancy. After our final term of biology when we studied reproduction we were sufficiently worldly to know that you didn't catch pregnancy from lavatory seats, like the VD at Victoria Station.

The reference to VD requires a word of explanation.

One bright day, a new doctor appeared on the scene, replacing an ancient dodderer who we reckoned was nearing his 100th birthday. Funnily enough he was called Dr Young and I think we thought he was the oldest person we were ever likely to meet this side of Heaven.

The new doctor was simply horrified about the navy blue knickers. NOT as you might think about the infrequent allocation of CLEAN knickers but by the fact that we were wearing navy blue fabric next to our skins. Suddenly we were made aware of the malicious harm that navy blue dye could inflict upon our bottoms and genitals. This, we supposed, in our anguished teenage innocence, was probably how people 'got VD'.

We weren't actually too sure about VD but we knew it must have reached pretty well epidemic proportions at Victoria Station because there was a large notice about it behind EVERY lavatory door.

It is extremely unusual to find a Headmistress showing promise as a *coiffeuse*.

Several times a week Miss Wilson would change into the old green jumper and we would be summoned for hair washing. Those selected for trial by water and Iscilma Shampoo queued up in Front 1 Bathroom in vest and pants, or combinations, and dressing-gowns. Presently Miss Wilson appeared, a large enamel basin was placed across the bath and large enamel jugs were filled with hot water. The first victim hung up her dressing-gown and was promptly seized by the back of the neck and her head dunked in the basin like a mop. Next Iscilma Shampoo was vigorously kneaded in. It seeped into the eyes and was breathed in by the nostrils, but we were not allowed flannels as protection. Dowsed with floods of too-hot water, gasping for air, blinded and stinging of eye, our hair was harshly wrung by hand and our heads thrust into the hand basin, which had been filled with lukewarm water and vin-egar, followed by a final cold rinse. Then vigorously towelled and painfully combed out, we were dispatched to Miss Wilson's room, there to lie on our elbows in front of her gas fire, or in summer, to the garden. The heat of the gas fire would cause bobbed hair to curl up at the ends and this always annoyed Miss Wilson, and we would be blamed for lying too close to the heat.

What is known as 'the common cold' was much *en évidence*.

The Headmistress spent much time and thought in a losing battle against colds, and she devised many methods against their spread, all totally unavailing. I myself never had less than four colds a term and this was about the norm, due I am sure to the tense atmosphere in which we all lived. Soon after my arrival

she had introduced nosebags in a bid to stop the spread
of infection. These were made of thick black cartridge
paper, stuffed with cotton wool sprinkled with oil of
eucalyptus and held in place by a piece of elastic
behind the ears and round the back of the head. These
were worn around the house and during prep, but not,
I think, during meals.

Many will remember a much-used method of putting paid to
a cold.

The remedy for the common cold was Throat Paint.
This was administered by the two sisters with very
long paint brushes. These brushes were identical with
the ones in the Art Room which were used for a colour
wash, for skies in particular. The throat brush was
plunged into a pot of evil-smelling purple fluid and as
you opened your mouth to its fullest extent, the brush
was thrust into your throat and the fluid was lashed
around your adenoids, tonsils and epiglottis. This
attack induced you to reel back, retch violently and
rush for the door. I must say though that in view of
the fact that it had a paralysing effect on your throat
for a good hour or so, it did relieve sore throat symptoms like nothing else in the world.

How sad that chilblains (and spots) should be such an apparently inseparable part of growing up.

The regimentation was extraordinary. Bells clanged
all day from the seven o'clock rising bell to the final
'Lights out' of the seniors. The winters were perishingly
cold. One antiquated coke-burning stove in the cloakroom heated a system of wide bore pipes, traversing
the four classrooms and dining-hall and the hot water
for two bathrooms, where the girls had their weekly
bath on a rota system. There was no heating in the
dormitories, which each housed a piano where we did
our half-hours of daily practising. Nearly everyone

had chilblains, but, of course, one had only to read Shakespeare to know that chilblains were part of winter!

In some schools the treatment handed out to girls seems to have been much harsher than that received by boys, obviously the weaker sex.

The next morning I got the first lesson of my life in tough living. I woke up feeling very poorly after the traumatic experience of the day before and, as I had been brought up to believe that bed was the only place if one was off-colour, I stayed in bed. The Lady Matron arrived and I explained the situation to her. She looked at me rather quizzically, but said nothing except that she would tell Miss Johnston. I expected breakfast, but none came and I felt neglected, hard-done-by and very, very homesick. I had reached the age of fifteen without ever having been away from Mother except for occasional visits to kind aunts, and nothing in girls' school stories had prepared me for a situation like this.

Presently with a jingle of chains Miss Johnston arrived. She always wore a long silver chain around her neck which gave warning of her approach, and we used to speculate as to whether she did this out of decency to warn us of her imminent arrival or whether she didn't realise what a help it was to all concerned. She came into my cubicle and sat down on the bed. 'What's the matter?' she said. I explained that I didn't feel at all well. A few probing questions and she had the heart of the matter. 'Well now, Rosemary,' she said. 'You can do one of two things. You can stay where you are, and everyone will be very nice to you but we shan't think much of you, or you can get up and come down and we will all respect you. Which will you do?'

What would you have done? I got up, shivering in the bitter cold, and went downstairs, and the only thing that surprises me now is that I was given a choice.

Illness was frowned upon, it simply wasn't the thing, and the worst possible crime you could commit in this field was to faint in Church. We had to go to early service, fasting. It was impressed upon us that, when cleaning our teeth, we must be careful not to swallow even a drop of water. The service was long and spent mostly on our knees, but heaven help you if you staggered out to the church porch or, worse still, collapsed in the pew. You were confined to your room for the rest of the day and told that if you were really ill it was the best place for you, and if you weren't, you deserved it. No food was forthcoming except by the good offices of friends. I remember on one occasion I was suffering from a feverish cold, or possibly 'flu. It was winter and as cold as the Cotswolds can be, and that is very cold indeed. I hung on as long as I could, alternately shivering and burning, but at last I took myself down to the study and asked Miss Johnston if I could go to bed. She looked at me coldly. 'Why?' she demanded. 'My head aches and I can't get warm,' I whimpered. I have never forgotten her reply. 'Why don't you skip?' she said.

The only time I ever saw Miss Johnston concerned about our health was one spring term when she decided (and I can only suppose she had been reading Nicholas Nickleby) that brimstone and treacle would be good for our systems and proceeded to mix a huge bowl of the nauseous stuff. We had to line up, for three mornings running, and file past the bowl picking up a teaspoon en route and helping ourselves to a dollop of the ghastly stuff. I managed somehow to evade this on the first two mornings, but Nemesis caught up with me on the third day when Miss Johnston realised there was one teaspoon left over and search parties were sent out.

The following episode will assist those who doubt the efficacy of prayer to adjust their views.

I once swallowed a shilling and ran screaming along the top corridor. When the nuns eventually got out of me what I had done, I was immediately put to bed while the two school doctors were summoned. They prescribed cotton-wool sandwiches, mashed potato and rice pudding, and milk drinks and nothing else, until the coin reappeared. I was to use the commode until it did. This diet was rigidly adhered to for four days, until the reappearance, and I was at last allowed OUT OF BED! During the first night of my 'confinement' several nuns at a time were heard praying outside my bedroom door: lengthy litanies were said, many decades of the rosary and a variety of prayers and incantations in Latin were also to be heard. Of course, as usual the 'Lord looks after his own'.

12

Leave-takings ·

For new girls, the arrival at a boarding school for the first time was a daunting experience and even in succeeding terms, when the pleasures and perils of the place were known (the latter probably not so frightening after all), the feeling of depression sometimes persisted.

Now, while staying at Minchinhampton, I had been told of a girls' boarding school nearby which sounded to me like all the books of Angela Brazil rolled into one. It was called Bussage House and was run by Miss Beale, a niece of the great Miss Beale of Cheltenham College, with a partner, Miss Johnston. It was small, only thirty-three girls, all boarders, and was housed in a country house in a most beautiful part of the Cotswold Hills.

'It's Bussage House or nowhere,' I said firmly and Bussage House it was. Mother wrote off straight away for the prospectus and back it came with a letter saying there was just one vacancy for the coming term and if I wanted it we had better buck up because term started on January 18th and it was now well into the second week of the new year. By this time I was all keyed up and ready to be the Nicest Girl in the Fifth or the Naughtiest Girl in the School, whichever seemed most appropriate when I arrived.

In spite of all our haste I was two days late in getting

to school because Mother, for some reason, couldn't come with me and it was not deemed suitable that I should travel alone, so my journey was put off until I could accompany a party of small boys, including my cousin, Anthony Wagner. They were returning to Beaudesert Park, the prep school at Minchinhampton to which three of my cousins went and where Uncle Alfie was the school doctor.

We met under the clock at Paddington, a couple of dozen little boys in grey tweed knickerbocker suits, one harassed assistant master and me in my mauve. I was to be put off at a small station called Brimscombe, where I was to be met, while they went on to Stroud.

When the moment came to say goodbye to Mother I felt ghastly, but I couldn't cry because of the boys. Anthony was already feeling the stigma of having his female cousin attached to the party at all, and I think he would have died of shame if I had dissolved into tears.

The journey took about two hours and the short January day was over when the train stopped at Brimscombe. Leaving the boys and the warm, lighted railway carriage was like leaving a liner for a small leaky boat and I stood there shivering in the bitter cold, clutching my overnight case, with my spirits at a very low ebb. Out of the darkness there emerged a quaint little figure wearing a short tweed coat, breeches and stockings who announced shyly that she was the Lady Gardener and that the cab was in the station yard.

The cab was old and musty, and so was the horse. We set forth in the darkness and seemed to be travelling vertically, so steep was the hill. The Lady Gardener was silent, and so was I, having just decided that the whole idea of boarding school was what Mother used to call 'One of Rosemary's mistakes', and trying to face the fact that it was now too late to do anything about it. How snug, how glamorous, that dull hotel

Leaving the warm lighted railway carriage, shivering in the bitter cold,
my spirits at a very low ebb . . .

in Notting Hill Gate now seemed. How absolutely necessary to my peace of mind was the presence of Mother. As for Angela Brazil, I felt convinced that she'd got it all wrong.

Up and up we crawled. I could no longer feel my feet. The darkness and the cold pressed round us like a wet blanket and sneaky little draughts blew up my brown-stockinged legs. At last after what seemed hours the horse suddenly stopped and the Lady Gardener said, 'We're here.'

And, arrived at school, it was not long before a girl would find herself faced with a time-table, of which the following (with explanations) is a good example.

Routine Called by bell at 6.30 a.m. (Silence all night and still silence!)

Breakfast 7.30. Bread and butter and coffee.

Chapel 8.15. 8.45 Free exercise in playground if fine, slides on ice in winter.

Lessons 9 a.m. The 3 R's and usual subjects. Algebra and Geometry, French and German, Sewing, Drawing and Painting, Singing, Piano and Violin (many music cubicles for practice), Dancing and Deportment including Court Curtsey, Swimming Baths and Gymnasium.

Drill daily.

Break 10.30 Bread and butter, milk for those on Doctor's orders.

Lessons 10.45 till Noon.

Mid-day Dinner 12.30. Usually meat and two veg. Resurrection Pie on Saturdays! No soup or fish. Suet Puddings (putty and varnish or Bugs in the Bolster), Jam tart, Milk puddings.

Games 1.15. Tennis, Cricket, Rounders, Hockey, Net Ball, Croquet, and/or Walks.

Lessons 2.30 to 4.30.

Tea 5 p.m. Before which the Chaplain conducted a short service of the lesson and prayers. Grace was sung accompanied on the harmonium. *Talking* was allowed during meals. We sat on hard wooden backless forms at trestle tables. Bread and butter, cake (jam on bread twice a week).

Cloisters In the short time before meals and after having brushed hair and tidied up, we repaired to the Cloisters, stone floor and stone pillars, where we promenaded round and round, arm-in-arm with chosen friends, anti-clock-wise for some unknown reason, which Freud no doubt could have explained!, till the bell rang for complete silence and for us to ascend the stairs in twos to the Assembly Room. Here we joined our particular Form line. A bell rang and, to a rousing tune on the piano, we marched along corridors to Dining Hall. We were certainly regimented!

Prep 6 p.m. till half an hour before bedtime, except on Saturdays, when we had dancing, partnering one another.

Good manners and polite behaviour should properly be taught in the home, largely by example, but, to cover possible deficiencies and to make all clear, one school issued, many years ago now, some very useful 'Etiquette Notes'.

When opening or closing a door the handle should be completely but quietly turned and the door closed without the least rattle.

The handkerchief should be used as noiselessly as possible and never examined after use.

In public baths; in dormitories; in bedrooms; or on any occasion in which necessity obliges young persons to make their toilet in the presence of others, they should see that perfect propriety characterises their behaviour. 'Let your modesty be known to all.'

The lips should be closed while eating. Neither should you speak, until you can do so with perfect ease. If addressed while eating, sufficient time should be taken to quietly dispose of your food before replying.

Do not blow on soup and tea in order to cool it.

Insolent, haughty and bold expressions indicate a proud and overbearing nature.

When passing mistresses or visitors, a slight inclination of the head should be made. The bow should be a graceful bend or an inclination of the head, not a hasty movement or a stiff jerk. 'Good Morning' or 'Good Afternoon' should be said.

Umbrellas are left in the Hall when making a visit.

Never throw articles out of a window.

Don't take any tool to cheese straws – pick up in fingers of right hand.

A young lady should never wear black patent leather shoes. They reflect one's undergarments.

When a young lady has occasion to find herself alone in a room, she should be sure always to have a duster with her. Then, if a young man enters, she can be busily engaged and move quickly around the room, thus avoiding any close encounters which would not be seemly.

Should a young lady go to a party or ball, she should always have about her person a telephone directory or other large book. Then, if a lift home in a car or carriage was proffered and it became necessary for the young lady to sit on the young gentleman's knee, because of crowding, then the book should first be placed on the gentleman's knee, before seating herself, thus avoiding any embarrassment to either.

No lapse in good behaviour or diligent work went unnoticed.

Good and bad, reward and punishment were strong features of school life. Our sins and virtues were picked upon by the staff and recorded by a system of stars and stripes. We received stripes for such offences as talking in the passage, talking on the stairs, talking after lights, talking after the bell for Prayers, not strip washing, forgetting to go to a music lesson, forgetting to put on blue knickers for Greek dancing. Stars, more hard to come by, were earned for things like good English/History/Geography essay, French dictation, maths, art, dancing, gym and occasionally obscurer virtues like 'showing courage in the face of temptation'. Four stripes or more a week meant some form of punishment; not being able to watch a hockey match (that suited me very well), missing sweets for a week or learning a chunk of poetry. More than four stripes and you were given what was deemed a more serious punishment. I remember two senior rebels who competed for most stripes in a week. They both managed about fourteen and were forbidden to go to any concerts, theatres, or other entertainment, for the rest of the term.

Four or more stars meant tea in the town. On the rare occasions that this reward came to me I found it less desirable than anticipated. Five or six of us, perhaps deadly enemies, with nothing in common but our stars, would walk, hatted and demure, to a refined little cafe where we were treated to scones, jam and those coconut iced cakes in violent colours. The real luxury was sauntering slowly back to prep and, unrestrained, being able to gaze at length into the fantasy world of the chemist shop window; powders, puffs, scent sprays, soaps lay all year round on a bed of tinsely stuff. These frivolous things pepped me up with a smug feeling of revival, for never were we allowed, in four years, to actually visit a shop. One moment in front of them after a star tea and, with renewed vigour, I was better able to re-apply myself to the Unification of Italy.

Our stars and stripes were revealed to the school at Saturday morning Prayers. As few girls in the school went through a week dodging at least one star or stripe, this was necessarily a lengthy business. Form by form we stood up, each girl's name was called and she was forced to say what the week had earned her. I remember the feeling of dread if I had a collection of bad stripes. It began on a Friday night. By Saturday morning I felt so sick I could not eat. I was rigid through the hymn, the prayer, almost voiceless, when at last my name was called. The common run of stripes, unless they were numerous, were not usually commented upon. But when a stripe triggered off a bout of anger in Miss Barrows she would first fix you with a long incredulous stare. Round her the semi-circle of staff rose from their lethargy and gazed sadly into the space somewhere short of your eyes, while the rest of the school would almost tangibly brace themselves for an enjoyable battle. It would go something like this:

Miss Barrows	Angela Huth?
Me	Stripe; frittering away my time in musical appreciation; Miss Jones [the donor].
Miss Barrows	FRITTERING AWAY YOUR TIME IN MUSICAL APPRECIATION? [Her voice maintained the incredulity of her stare.]
Me	Yes, Miss Barrows.
Miss Barrows	FRITTERING . . .
Me	Yes, Miss Barrows.

Long, long terrible silence was followed by hot explosion covering, not only the immediate misdemeanour, but the sins one had supposed most jealously guarded; a stripping bare of one's soul before staff and pupils. Humiliating, to say the least. But we were a school of stiff upper lips and not many succumbed to tears or blushes.

At the end of the holidays taking leave of home has painful memories for many.

—My recollections of boarding school begin with memories of Victoria Station where, with sinking heart and butterflies in my stomach, I was to meet up with the rest of the girls, say goodbye to my mother and father whilst trying to hold back the tears, and board the waiting train, waving to my parents until they were out of sight while the train moved inexorably on its journey to Eastbourne. Of course, as the years went by and one settled down and made friends, this became much less painful; however, the sight of the name of the last station before Eastbourne – Polegate – always triggered off mixed feelings of dread and anticipation at the new term ahead.

—I remember the dreadful sinking feeling as the end of the holidays drew nigh (akin to the visit to the dentist each hols – 'It's a long journey, I needn't panic yet . . .'); the attempts to swallow the tears at the hour of parting, knowing that my parents felt the same, but accepting without question that this was something that had to be done. (My own daughter is much brighter and in that position would have demanded a good reason WHY she had to go away; however things are so different now – boarding school for her is financially out of the question and she would probably enjoy it anyhow, such are the perversities of life.) The unpacking of the trunk, checking the clothes list and the fear of something being wrong or missing, though everything had been carefully gone through at home.

—Our term really started with a tearful parting from one's parents on Victoria Station, when we were escorted onto the specially chartered Schools Train taking all the children back to their various schools in Kent – there were a large number of them in those days. Having found our compartment, we were not allowed into the corridor lest a male eye from a spotty thirteen-year-old looked in our direction. Should some poor unfortunate find it necessary to whisper that she wished to 'go to the end of the corridor', she had to be chaperoned both ways! Having arrived at the school and been told which room we would be in there was a mad rush up the stairs to secure the best bed in the room – usually the one nearest the window.

—The trunk was bought, the uniform ordered and bit by bit it arrived and September seemed to be advancing too, September 1930. What a special smell the new trunk had, it was stiff and the lid creaked on opening, the top tray had loops for the fingers and small keys were tied on. Packing started, and the list was checked. Cash's names were stitched on to everything, and items were tried on. How heavy the velour hat seemed, with the school ribbon of cerise and navy blue, and how rough the flannel blazer felt on bare arms, there was a badge on the pocket and the stern school motto: Facta non Verba. Two gymslips, one for summer wear, and the white silk dress with long sleeves and flat collar and white silk gloves, this outfit was for dancing classes, summer processions, big Church feasts and concerts. Late September and the brown lisle stockings were on, the flat-heeled brown leather shoes, a navy blue serge dress, a thick navy blue top coat, gloves and velour hat. We were off to York. In the train I read a school story about girls playing hockey and having feasts in the 'dorms'. At York a mistress was waiting

to escort the party to Harrogate. The convent boarding school 'for the daughters of gentlemen', so I had
seen it described. I finished the school story in the
train and that was the last one I read for months.
Taxis took us to the convent, just outside Harrogate,
and we stepped into the cool hall. Immediately I
noticed the special smell: polish, disinfectant, new
trunks in the gym, and a warmer leathery smell. On
to the school refectory where, at the sound of a bell,
all sat down and with a lay sister presiding the
maids served a meal of cold meat, beetroot, bread
and butter and stewed fruit. There was subdued
talking, but the nun in charge told us that meals
would be henceforth eaten in silence, unless there
was a special feast day, or someone had a birthday.
After the meal we had to find our names on the
dormitory lists, with names like Blessed Sacrament
(dormitory), St Angela's, St Joseph's and so on.
There were some ninety-five girls boarding at that
time.

And on to the poignant last day at school, the leaving, the
regrets, the memories, the nostalgic returns and, almost without exception, the feelings of gratitude and love.

—And now the years had come and gone. There is
always an emptiness when one rises for 'God Save
the King', and the show's over, and it's Home
Again; but for me it was an aspect fraught with
special desolation and apprehension. What lay
ahead? What renewed developments of past anguish
and fear? To what was I returning with the walled
and turreted refuge of school gone for ever?
    The last evening – the last morning. School
Prayers. You could always tell who was leaving by
the gradual cessation of those senior voices which
were the usual mainstay of high notes and difficult
passages.

Only the lesser voices were left now to tackle,

> Let Thy Father Hand be shielding
> Those who here will meet no more.

How often we had sung it, mourning the departure of our divinities, our heroines. But now it was *us*! It was for *us* the school was singing now. It was upon *us* the doors of that passionately loved place were now closing for the last time.

Nay, we even heard them shut *and we were outside*, as the carefree voices of our happy juniors soared up to the most famous high note in the annals of the schools of England,

> Tho-o-o-ose returning, make more faithful
> Tha-a-a-an before.

—I crept back for consolation one day in the holidays. At first I only noticed the ghostly, almost sepulchral hush of the school building emptied of its pupils. And then I was assailed, almost intoxicated, by that 'unforgettable, unforgotten' typically girls' school smell – a compounded whiff of old and much polished linoleum, a burnt offering from the cookery-class kitchens, something even more sinister from the stinks lab and the sweat-impregnated rubber of generations of gym shoes. Now Forty Years On, it is still vivid in my nostrils, and in my heart!

—The last three years were the best of all my school life – good friends, good lessons, good games, good training for life, and a scholarship to Oxford before I left.

After starting to walk home on my last day, I had to return for something I had left in my desk. The school was still open, but there was nobody about. No one in the classrooms, or on the stairs or in the passages. Just stillness: and silence: and emptiness.

I went into my form room and over to my desk, and the lid made its familiar bang as I shut it. The form room was so empty. I could not bear the silence and the stillness. Only a butterfly was beating its wings against the glass, and I let it out of the window.

Then I turned and left the room. Down the stairs, along the wide corridor and out of the main entrance.

I was feeling very sad as I walked home over the North Road, through the Bull Park, and across the Town Moor. My schooldays were over.

List of contributors

C. Adison

J. Baldwin

P. Barker

R. Bowmer

T. Buckle

S. M. Buckley

M. Cadogan

J. Cant

V. Chaumeton

E. Clifton-Mogg

P. Cook

M. Cordrey

L. Cower

S. Crabtree

R. Daubney

P. Day

B. Deadman

C. de Pertinez

K. M. Eastham

D. M. Edwards

E. R. Evans

S. Fazakerley

J. Frazer-Smith

B. K. Gallie

G. Hamel

E. B. Hamilton

J. Harwood

H. R. Holden

A. Huth

H. A. Kay

V. Lobb

E. Manners

K. L. Miles

D. M. Miller

W. Nethercott

J. Norman

L. North

V. Perrin

E. B. Pidgeon

J. Pierson

B. Priest

R. Reeves

A. Scott

M. Selby-Green

V. Sergeant

J. Sharp

A. Smith

S. G. Smith

C. Snell

M. Spence

S. Taylor

P. M. Teage

R. Weir

Fontana Paperbacks: Non-fiction

Fontana is a leading paperback publisher of non-fiction. Below are some recent titles.

- [ ] THE LIVING PLANET David Attenborough £8.95
- [ ] SCOTLAND'S STORY Tom Steel £4.95
- [ ] HOW TO SHOOT AN AMATEUR NATURALIST Gerald Durrell £2.25
- [ ] THE ENGLISHWOMAN'S HOUSE
       Alvilde Lees-Milne and Derry Moore £7.95
- [ ] BRINGING UP CHILDREN ON YOUR OWN Liz McNeill Taylor £2.50
- [ ] WITNESS TO WAR Charles Clements £2.95
- [ ] IT AIN'T NECESSARILY SO Larry Adler £2.95
- [ ] BACK TO BASICS Mike Nathenson £2.95
- [ ] POPPY PARADE Arthur Marshall (ed.) £2.50
- [ ] LEITH'S COOKBOOK
       Prudence Leith and Caroline Waldegrave £5.95
- [ ] HELP YOUR CHILD WITH MATHS Alan T. Graham £2.95
- [ ] TEACH YOUR CHILD TO READ Peter Young and Colin Tyre £2.95
- [ ] BEDSIDE SEX Richard Huggett £2.95
- [ ] GLEN BAXTER, HIS LIFE Glen Baxter £4.95
- [ ] LIFE'S RICH PAGEANT Arthur Marshall £2.50
- [ ] H FOR 'ENRY Henry Cooper £3.50
- [ ] THE SUPERWOMAN SYNDROME Marjorie Hansen Shaevitz £2.50
- [ ] THE HOUSE OF MITFORD Jonathan and Catherine Guinness £5.95
- [ ] ARLOTT ON CRICKET David Rayvern Allen (ed.) £3.50
- [ ] THE QUALITY OF MERCY William Shawcross £3.95
- [ ] AGATHA CHRISTIE Janet Morgan £3.50

You can buy Fontana paperbacks at your local bookshop or newsagent. Or you can order them from Fontana Paperbacks, Cash Sales Department, Box 29, Douglas, Isle of Man. Please send a cheque, postal or money order (not currency) worth the purchase price plus 15p per book for postage (maximum postage required is £3).

NAME (Block letters) _____

ADDRESS _____

_____

_____